JUST BE,

THERE IS ONLY ONE LOVE

Just Be

There is Only One Love

AN INSPIRATIONAL WORK BY:

COLLEEN ANN NUGENT

Published by HN Books, LLC,

Colleen Ann Nugent and James Hockenberry

HN Books, LLC, P.O. Box 4214, New Windsor, New York 12553, USA

Copyright © 2016, published @2021 by Colleen Ann Nugent

Endpapers, interior, and cover illustrations by HN Books, LLC

All rights reserved. No part of this book may be reproduced, scanned, or distributed in any printed or electronic form without permission.

Please do not participate in or encourage piracy of copyrighted materials in violation of the author's rights.

Purchase only authorized editions.

Library of Congress Cataloging-in-Publication Data Nugent, Colleen Ann

Just Be, There Is Only One Love /Colleen Ann Nugent

p. cm.

ISBN: 978-0-9915612-6-1 (paperback)
ISBN:978-0-9915612-7-8 (eBook)

1. Inspirational,
2. Spiritual,
3. Romance,
4. Humanity,
5. Philosophy,
6. Contemporary Literature,
7. Young Teen & Adult,
8 Psychology,
9 New Age

Printed in the United States of America

Book Design by HN Books,
LLC First private edition 2021 HN Books,
LLC, P.O. Box 4214, New Windsor, NY 12553 USA

DEDICATION

This book is dedicated to the notion of Immortality.

Just Be, There Is Only One Love
is meant to give everyone; all ages, all walks of life,
living in every geography, a sense of immortality in this life.

To be loved, is to also be remembered.
To be remembered is to become immortal.
My definition of loving is to; create happiness,
spread joy and make wonderful memories.

May you all find your own way, to become immortal
in your lifetime.

CONTENTS

Introduction xiii

1 There are All Types of Love 1
   (Explanation of Encompassing Aspects of One Universal Love)

2 Love of Friendship 31

3 The Wisdom of Love .47

4 Love Never Fails 63

5 Love of Self 85

6 Love of Humanity 103

7 In Love with Loving 115

8 The Hope in Love 127

9 Devoted to the Immortal 141

10 Soul Love The Greatest of Love 157

   Acknowledgements 167

Maternal Nature
Original is 20" x 16", acrylic on canvas

Maternal Nature happened because my cousin MaryAnn guided me in the remembrance of her Mom.

To MaryAnn, the painting evoked a feeling the nurturing and unconditional love present in the natural world, and the loving signs offered by our missing ones in heaven.

To me, it brings to notions to mind of our precious universe showing how beautiful it is, and how soul energy can never be extinguished.

Introduction

INTRODUCTION

Just Be, There Is Only One Love

Infinite power acts as tiny acts. This is my truth.

An infinite and universal truth that I wish to explain.

How to explain "the encompassing aspects of one universal love?"

To explain one universal love has taken centuries and countless minds. It is an all-encompassing group effort.

Many books have been written and many teachers teach the broader notion of universal love.

My God lives in my cells, I am but a vessel. This small book is a view of universal love written to explain (by my perceptions from this mortal vessel).

This writing was a complete challenge. I had never written anything, let alone an entire book on my thoughts.
These chapters include thoughts from reading books and absorbing teachings of religion and philosophy and art.

Just Be, is a true "labor of love". You see, my longtime and dear friend wrote a book, and I assisted in publishing the books through HN Books LLC. We attended many literary group meetings. I felt so "at home" Yet, something was missing, it was me! I knew I had this story in me. The idea came to me suddenly, but it began to bubble up and through my fingers, I wanted to write my thoughts on love.

This work is meant to be a series of thoughts explaining views on ten specific aspects of "Just Be". One distinct love. An explanation of my understanding of unconditional love.

As I searched for answers in books and on the internet, it seemed, no other author had intertwined religion, psychology, and philosophy. No one had woven the concepts together, or as one whole idea.

As I researched, I understood why.

Unconditional love is a large encompassing state of mind, requiring acts of trust and humility.

When I announced to my friends, my intent to write a book, no one blatantly exclaimed, "You are finally too crazy for me". Instead, they sent me sayings and quotes and ideas about life.

Just Be, There Is Only One Love is a group of good thoughts leading us on a path to the complete concept of an all-encompassing loving reality.

These chapters are a mix of contemplations on love, including views from contemporary literature and facts from history. Then passages written by my friends, a group of loving people, and the stories of their lives.

Love is organic just as the cells in our bodies. Love is mutative and grows generationally. Love is immortal; and something to be achieved.

This book is a creative work where I pushed on further and accumulated enough ideas to encompass the entire spectrum of love in one small book. (and in my lifetime!).

My thoughts here are a tribute to life. A tribute to the unconditionally loving people in this world.

Some passages are statements of hope and of surrender to love and to what life brings us all. Someone told me as she read this book seemed to be about death; or the process of letting go of life.

Do not concern yourself with death, it will come to every mortal.

This book is about making the most of life.

A thought I found in author Marianne Williamson's writings:

"Love is what we are born with. Fear is what we learn. The spiritual journey is the unlearning of fear and prejudices and the acceptance of love back in our hearts. Love is the essential reality and our purpose on earth. To be consciously aware of it, to experience love in ourselves and others, is the meaning of life.
Meaning does not lie in things.
Meaning lies in us."

Each of us truly has no choice whether we live with the good and the bad in the world. Both good and bad are ever present. Some passages are remembrance of good things and great love. One small passage are the words of a 14-year-old to her mother.

This book started as my attempt to get this ebullient idea out of my head, into complete thought, down on paper (old school joke!), and then finally into a book.

There are ideas from all kinds of religions (About 20 different and/or sects of major religions), most traditional and popular philosophy, modern day psychology and from those I affectionately
call "self-help guru's"

Each of the 10 chapters and 13 paintings are meant to tell a story of an opinion on love. A discussion of an aspect of love.

A how-to "Just Be" in love. As it progressed through time, this story became "battle hardened" by the friendships and loves in my own life.

The chapters describe ten aspects of one unconditional love. Each chapter represents one aspect of love. Every chapter depicting aspects of a divine relationship with love.
The ten aspects lead you directly to unconditional love.

All aspects of love are wonderful, love encompasses all.

As the beliefs filled the pages, many of the concepts came from what I read about the immortals (Immortals=God and all the infinite loving deities); literary contemporaries I have read throughout my life, and of course, my opinion of their thoughts.

My hope is to present you with an ever-pervasive illumination of loving thoughts.

My wish for you is to carry this book as life carries you through the joys and struggles to live and to die with dignity.
In different sections, you will see the different references to friends, most friends pop up more than once. I unabashedly, offered them immortality by becoming part of this book, for their guidance and contributions.

One thing is certain in every work I encountered, there is an infinite love everyone can access, and you just need to open your heart to new opportunities by using kind ways.
May your trip through the spectrum of love be all you desire and let your trip be entirely memorable as I wish your happiness to become permanent.

Chapter One

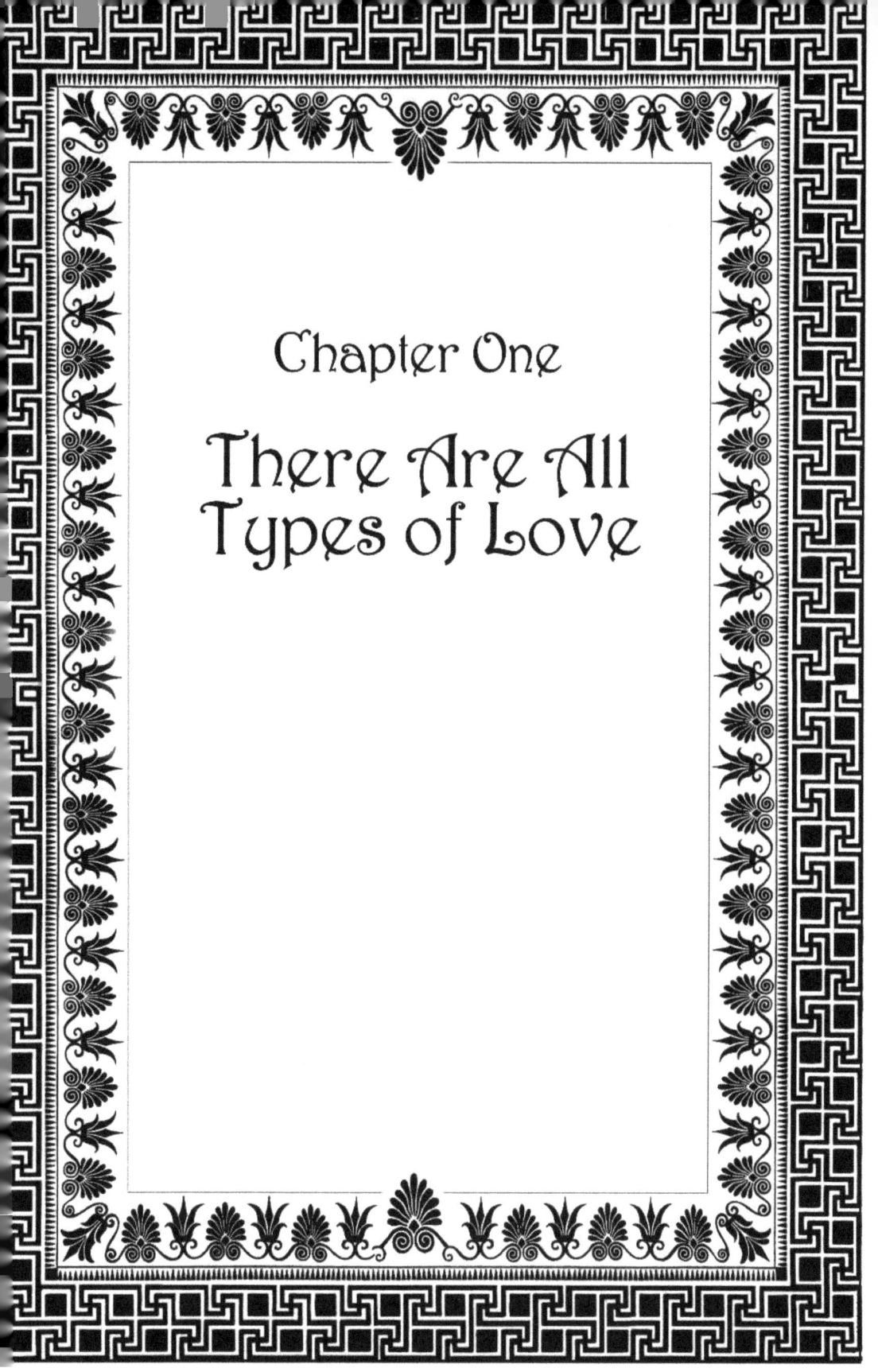

There Are All Types of Love

Cardinal on a Swing

Original is 6 ½" x 9" acrylic on canvas

For centuries, in many different cultures, the cardinal represents many beliefs.

Cardinals are known as a symbol of hope, healing, joy, rejuvenation, health, and celebration.
Some believe a cardinals' love is so profound, heaven sends them as signs of devotion from your loved ones.

The appearance of this bright red bird serves to remind us of our creators ever protective and watchful guidance. Tradition teaches this special bird also epitomizes exceptional people who are rare, energetic, and mindful of others.

Cardinals work diligently to find their soulmate.
They are monogamous, can live up to 15 years, and continue to take care of each other throughout their lives.

My painting is winter with a vibrant red male on a swing. He waits patiently to see his loved one so he can sooth her by singing a song.

> **NOTICE:**
>
> YOU ARE HEREBY ALLOWED TO BE HAPPY,
> TO LOVE YOURSELF, TO REALIZE YOUR WORTH,
> TO BELIEVE IN GREAT THINGS, AND TO BE TREATED
> WITH LOVE AND RESPECT

(found on the website: www.thehiyl.com)

This notion was something I found when I searched for affirmations you can recite for yourself every day. There are many free blogs and social media pages where you can read and enjoy positive and enlightening wisdom at your fingertips.

Do not ever stop your research into love. Keep a journal of all your findings and go back in six months and see how you feel about them then. You can gauge how much you have grown.

It is a magical feeling.

"One word frees us all of the weight and pain of life; that word is love" **–Sophocles**

This book is a book of love.
10 different aspects of the very same love.
Just Be, There Is Only One Love
This book is meant to convey the profound message of using kindness in every action. We will all prosper and accumulate moments of unconditional love. The goal of life is to endure everyday challenges using unconditional love for everything around you.

What is this book about?
I want to help you relate your spiritual understanding of Mother Earth with your practical understanding of nature on our Mother Earth. Unconditional love, God's love, is the universal force of life.

This force of life runs through every living being.
In our humanly struggles here on Mother Earth, greater growth results from greater struggles.

Growth through our ardent effort to continuously try, leads to a distinct strengthening of spirit and strengthening of our free will. This kind of growth will then lead to a sustaining fulfillment.

To learn to maintain your strength and to how to heal yourself will allow you to learn a way to sustain yourself through even the most arduous journeys.

Notice I did not say, know how to maintain your strength. No. I said learn to maintain and to heal first. You are not expected to maintain perfect levels of strength through everything. It is simply not possible.

Your first goal is to be ok, then you may try to help others.

Let us start out right.

Understanding is key to learning. Here it is:

No one is sent by accident to anyone.

We are all connected by a universal energy —
people, trees, animals, everything.

Believe this, Just Be...and you become more of it.

(I promise to use the rest of this book to explain this to you)

Let us discuss the written works here on Mother Earth. Specifically, the group of works called philosophy and self-help.

Lots of philosophers speak of "inner light."

First, let us assume "inner light" means "God within" or "true nature". Inner light shines forth from every sentient being.

This inner light can also be called your "essence", as it is organic, primal, and pure.
This essence is part of every living thing.

This is a planet of free will. A planet full of sentient beings. A sentient being is any living organism which can display it has thoughts and feelings. Every sentient being is trying to live its own life in peace and happiness.

I have read authors who tell you to shine so others can.

Here is a wonderful example: This passage is commonly mis-attributed to Nelson Mandela's 1994 Inaugural Address. It comes from the book 'A Return To Love' (1992) by Marianne Williamson

"...Our deepest fear is not that we are inadequate.
Our deepest fear is that we are powerful beyond measure. It is our light, not our darkness that most frightens us.
We ask ourselves, who am I to be brilliant, gorgeous, talented, fabulous?
Who are you not to be? You are a child of God.
Your playing small does not serve the world.
There is nothing enlightened about shrinking
so that other people won't feel insecure around you. We are all meant to shine, as children do.
We were born to make manifest the glory of God that is within us. It's not just in some of us; it's in everyone.
And as we let our own light shine, we unconsciously give other people permission to do the same.
As we are liberated from our own fear, our presence automatically liberates others."

There are All Types of Love
(Encompassing aspects of one universal love)

There can be another view here. Try to think of this using an alternative premise. My contribution is this thought: Please believe you should shine because you can. It is your gift to the world.

If you offer kindness and compassion and help when you can, you innately promote well-being in all those around you.
Your life becomes surrounded by warmth and love.

*   *   *

Choose your surroundings wisely.
Let all those around you shine their light at the same intensity. Do not succumb to those who hide behind your light.
Or those who may try to claim your light as their own.

Kindness and compassion will always lead to positive interactions.
In every situation, positive interactions lead directly to unconditional love.

Do not concern yourself if your path is a little different. You are here to live your own paradigm in consciousness.

A paradigm in consciousness can simply be described as a summary of your actual physical ability to perceive the reality happening in and around you. In other words, you are one being. Your being has a current consciousness.
You are one aspect of the collective consciousness of Mother Earth. One light in the sea of lights. One fiber in the tapestry of community. Each light is, and every fiber becomes,
the unique and true gift to share with humanity.

Awakened and in grateful service,
you are here to live your own gift. This gift bestowed on you to help this great Mother Earth and all its sentient beings.

To discuss the notion of "sentient beings" a little further, anything sentient is aware. Awareness creates a distinct value. All living creatures have their own place in the great ecosystem of this world. Each living creature helps to create our physical living environment. Everyone and every creature is born with something to contribute to our Mother Earth. To follow this concept further, everyone and every being can be nurtured into showing their true potential.
Please believe each being and each person has a unique gift.

To use the analogy of an intricately woven tapestry, your life should be a collection of unique fibers woven into you as a gift.
Each fiber/loving person in your life creates your unique and impeccably designed life's fabric. Tend to the weave of your fabric well. Weave only with the best quality threads, threads which are supple and strong, utterly natural.

If you have learned the laws of karmic attraction (or simply know the laws of physical attraction), if you choose to use your innate gift for good, how can anything bad happen to you?

Here is a positive and joyful piece of advice:

Attract positive thought and experiences by living in the moment
and choosing every moment to project kindness and love.

The love brought forth from compassion, the love brought about by togetherness, then creates a feeling of oneness and well-being in individuals, communities, and countries.

This well-being then creates respect and tolerance of other points of view and in modes of expression. This then leads to exciting and encompassing joy and eventually, feelings lead to loving.

This kind of love is complete.
This unconditional love state, this special kind of love,
needs only acceptance to exist.

It has been said "familiarity breeds contempt".
This idea may be true at a base and superficial level. Please believe, if you view life as a big competition and choose to compete at life,
you will always find something with which to compete.

If you flow along with life, always careful to follow your own direction, and weave your own fabric, this safe passage allows you to grow patience and tolerance.

If you need to respect everyone's space and you learn to respect the individuality of every person, you will eventually adorn your fabric with strong threads of family and with golden threads of friendship throughout life.
One day, you will just begin to see why you should just love them all.
Each one.
Differently.
But you will be in love with them all, still the same.

A further discussion on the concept of loving every sentient being, we are one with all creatures on Mother Earth.

Sadly, we must admit, humans have forgotten to listen to the animals and forgotten to heed to the signs and signals sent to us by Mother Earth.

Other living things live in peace and enjoy life as best they can.

Animals use their instincts to live as well as they can and be content. You only must see a kitten asleep in a flowerpot, to realize it is easy to become happy. The kitten enjoys everything new and lives to be happy.

Some animals join when needed, and others forge out alone when necessary.

Animals live in freedom and harmony with Mother Earth.

Let's talk about using your "spirit" as a gift to the world. This is a world of free will. Both good and evil are very real. Good and evil are the universe achieving balance. This balance can be most elusive…

"A spiritual warrior must be comfortable in both the dark and the light, knowing both conditions are reflections of the other.
Yet... love is the energy which unites all things. If you love someone or even a animal, it is extremely hard to see the differences between your own needs and theirs."

A spiritual warrior is someone who deals with things happening outside their ability to control them, with dignity and grace.

Unfortunately, in life, there are good situations and bad situations. Things sometimes outside your immediate control such as a bad marriage/good divorce, long lived health/ short term sickness, and ultimately life/death.

The goal must be to be careful to weave thoughts of gratitude in every day. To live in gratitude every day.
To enjoy weaving a strong, supple life fabric,
using unique threads of friendship and loving kindness.
When your fabric is strong, the bad times become just part of the weave. Painful events can no longer ruin or corrupt the weave of fabric. Only mortality can stop the weaving.
To live in spirit is to become immortal here on Mother Earth.

Here is a great story about loving.
"I've never found love to be anything short of Magic...completely unexpected, never predictable and always wildly enchanting."

My friend who has been with me through school and various jobs sent this thought. We have watched each other learn, grow and prosper in love. This thought is an explanation of what love has meant to her. Thank you, my friend! You explained it well.

We grew up in a wonderful time of existence. The magic of the 1960's is a powerful way to view the world- a world where love is magic. Our America was at war. We were losing our young people to war. Yet, it grew into a time of love and of exploration. New types of music, new technology, new exposure to other cultures.

For all of you too young to remember these things, I have listed their source here. Enjoy learning some great 1960's creative works.

There is a song by Steppenwolf called "Magic Carpet Ride" If you do not remember the song, please look it up. "Close your eyes girl. Look inside girl. Let the sound take you away."

Or maybe you are too young to remember a TV show about the two-thousand-year-old genie released from the bottle by the astronaut, (aired on TV from 1965-1970 called "I Dream of Jeannie").

My clearest intention, for each of you, is to have a great ride on the "magic carpet ride" of life.

Now let us discuss how people form friendships or, to use our ongoing analogy, how people weave the fabric of their life.

When you first meet someone,
if you offer your introduction in a loving way, they must choose to love back...or to shy away.

Either way, you have a positive interaction.

In the very least, if you offer your greeting in a loving way, they will remember you as a kind person. If they choose to shy away,
they will leave with the memory of your kindness.

Please never be afraid to love.
Please never be afraid to say goodbye.

Some people are not meant to stay in your life. Each has an individual path.

Sometimes, the very thing you need to learn is to let someone go. Sometimes, you need to learn to grow on your own. Sometimes, you give people the strength they need to grow for themselves.

The people who stay are meant to become part of your fabric. The people too shy to stay, have their own growing to do. All situations are not your battle. Only some are. If you stay close to your real essence, if you live in your own truth, the path will be clear.

Please learn to stay true to yourself.

Love, Happiness and Peace...all lead back to Love.

Unconditional love contains both happiness and peace. Love leads back to love. Isn't that simple?
Everyone strives for a perfect balance.

A perfect moment will last through eternity.

This life is made of a string of "perfect moments". Your fabric of life becomes stronger each time you intricately weave some beautiful threads into it. Each golden thread filled with these perfect moments.

It is important to learn all the different pathways to love. One of the unlimited number of pathways is religion. Often, people do not believe in the same religion, yet they still can value each other.

It is said there are 5500 different religious paths here on Mother Earth today. Some people do not believe in religion at all. Each person is free to choose his/her individual path. If they're heading to love, it really does not matter. Only unconditional love matters.

To learn the concepts of many religions is to learn about a human man who attained immortality in his one lifetime here on Mother Earth.

In all religious teachings, you will read about continuous feelings of love and kindness toward others. The belief is to love unconditionally, and this will promote inner happiness, peace and serenity.

My wish for you is to find the joy in giving to others, while the work of giving replenishes your soul at the same time.

This everyday world has struggles. Life is sometimes inconvenient and even downright mean.

" If you want to change how you do life, you must change how you view life"

After finding the to-do list added here, I realized there were more items to include. Balance should always be our goal.

A To-Do List for Every Day

Be kind and find ways to do kind things
Learn and grow from what you cannot control Let the flow of life take you gently to your destiny
Revel in all your blessings! Every day, be thankful for the day Listen to your inner voice/ intuition/ gut instinct
Just Be, instill calmness around yourself Give and share our love wherever possible
Pass this on- share encouragement with others

If you carry out your to-do list every day, you weave your threads into existence, which then become your fabric.

Your fabric will keep you warm and comfortable.
You can even adorn it with colorful beads of beautiful moments.

The way life works is everything born is eventually going to experience death. Be comforted in the physical fact: matter may change, but energy is never extinguished.

Though life may be impermanent,
beautiful happy moments become immortal.

You always have the love and fond memories you grew in your heart.

It never ceases, never fades.

One beautiful and gracious soul, Mahatma Gandhi wrote these words as an offering to the world. I thank him for it. These words are precious.

To think this human man lived and left this for our world- what an outstanding gift. Please enjoy!

I offer you peace. I offer you love.
I offer you friendship. I see your beauty.
I hear your need.
I feel your feelings.
My wisdom flows from the highest Source. I salute that Source in you. Let us work together. For unity and peace."

- Gandhi's prayer for peace

The mindful expression, opinions, actions and interpretations of this blessed prayer for peace are exactly why I chose to write this book.

The illumination of the many aspects of love, each with a unique nuance, leading to one unconditional love.

In this one passage shows love of humankind, the love of human spirit, the love of each other and, finally, the hope of one day we can all be as loved as we need.

A book about love, especially unconditional love would not be complete without including the deep emotional bonds which comes from loving all creatures, but specifically, those we take into our home as pets.

In a world sometimes too cruel,
to know you have made a loving difference for another living creature,
to know you created
safety and comfort for a creature is the greatest of gifts- to yourself
Lovers of furry creatures
do not leave their animals out in the heat or in the cold,
and when they lie down at night,
our beloved furry friends are on the bed or at least snuggled close by,
safe from the dark and dangers that roam in the night.

Here is a basic concept from biology. Physical love can be expressed in biological terms. The biology of love is as follows:

"We are made by love" "We are made of love" and "We are made for love."

Isn't it a wonderful thought?

I always say when two people love each other deeply, they create the most beautiful children.

If you think of love in this way, you are made by this love,
then how can you possibly deny it for yourself?

You are entitled to it.
You deserve it and it is part of you and part of your balance.

You are part of the grand scheme
and play a part in the universe. You are important to the world. Every person impacts other lives. Every person.

Are you holding back from love because you believe, somewhere inside yourself, somehow you do not deserve it?
Every sentient being deserves love. Your task is not to seek love,
but merely seek and find all the barriers within yourself that you have built up against it.
– Rumi

Does Rumi think love can be conquered by conquering your inner self?

If you can conquer your inner fear, will you find love? Try it and find out! If you are made of love and made for love, then what holds you back from loving?

This, my friends, is what we are learning every day...

If all the philosophers, alchemists and scientists are correct, then we may be convinced immortal love
flows freely in the universe.

Love flows just as water does and it permeates
just as your breath does, always present but unseen.

Love is meant to flow through every living being, every creature, every animal and every plant
(and yes, it is proven plants do react to stimulus and nurturing). Love is meant to further our life, just as air and water do.
Please believe that you will survive but you cannot fully live, without love.

To explain Rumi, one must learn of Persia. Persia is an ancient country now known as Iran. Rumi is known in modern times as a famous Persian philosopher who gave our world an arsenal of positive beliefs.

To continue the discussion of many paths and types of religion, Rumi was known to be a Sufi Mystic.
A mystic is a "holy man". A mortal man who devotes himself to seeking God with every waking breath.

In other religions, he might have been called a monk, a yogi, a priest or rabbi, or maybe a nun (for a woman) or a brother (for a man).

For us, he is simply a servant of God here on Mother Earth.

Interestingly, a person who is a Sufi strives for Ihsan (perfection of worship). Can you imagine it is not enough to live for God, but further, you need to learn to be a perfect worshipper?

More pointedly to our intent here, Ihsan is to "worship God as if you see Him; if you can't see Him, surely He sees you" (from the Hadith).
Sufis regard the person who lived to be known as the Prophet Muhammad is described a primary perfect man who exemplifies the morality of God.

There is only one God. Unconditional love leads to God.
Kindness and loving ways lead to God.

Equally of interest, Buddhists also believe the Buddha was a mortal man who attained total and unconditional spiritual enlightenment during the earthly lifetime of his physical body.

Furthermore, the Christian religion is based on the love and devotion of the Son of God, Jesus Christ. Jesus was a child born through the immaculate conception of Mary, who was the wife of Joseph. Jesus lived and roamed on Mother Earth according to the Scriptures written after his death.

Christians believe Jesus Christ to be the true Son of God. All those who follow the path of Jesus are to be redeemed before our Lord. Buddhists, Muslims and Sufi Mystics are three examples of our human body/being's ability to attain immortality. Isn't it a wonderful thought?

This one concept allows death to never happen. Only life in the physical body changes form.
It changes to "immortal life" or in other words, it will change to the place of "immortal love". Immortal love will give you an immortal life.
Unconditional love or immortal love is something to look forward to!

These devotees of God share their light. They become "light givers". Rumi gave his light through his teachings, to shine through his words for centuries.
Please use the fibers of Rumi to adorn your fabric. A soul whose thread became of the highest quality.

When used to weave your fabric of firm truths,
you will be glad to have Rumi's advice and strength.

This is another human shining his light for others to embrace. Rumi's words are firmly woven into my fabric of love for life itself.
His words can change the way we view our daily world and Mother Earth.

"Love is the bridge
between You and Everything"
-Rumi

Love has the power to change anything
as well as nurture growth in one's self.

"Love can be as deep as an ocean or as shallow as a drop, but it still has the strength to overcome."

Isn't this sentiment beautiful?

Love can have great power. Love can take many forms. It can be superficial, or it can be deep-rooted. Love is pervasive and ever-present. Love can nurture and love can sustain.

My girlfriend from elementary school kept sending me her thoughts and words coming out of her head because we have loved each other since we were little children. We have a deep love of friendship. We think of each other as quite special, no matter what anyone else has to say. It is so fun!

May your loving ways patch the bare spots and fill the holes in your life's fabric. May your love be a drop of water, or a thread of life, but still be supple and strong.

Let your love be strong enough, you want to share it.

Growing up in the 1960's and 1970's was magical, innocent time.

The emerging music, the fashion, this beautiful country called America... we were of the flowers, we were star shine, we were moonlight...everything was possible through love.

"Love is the flowers, You've got to let grow"
(from the song "Mind games" by John Lennon and sung by the Beatles)

Love is the truth. Love needs to be nurtured. Love needs to be regarded with an open mind and an open heart. The lover and the loved must be equally nurtured. If you give love, promise yourself you will allow yourself to receive love too.
To use an analogy of a plant, If you add too much water (tears/drama) the plant will drown.

If you neglect the plant, it will not blossom, unless it is a Christmas cactus.

Love is the same with people. Most people need to be nurtured continually.
Though, if you meet the right kind of love, you will be nurtured by strength of the love alone. You will be nurtured by the unconditional love of another.

This kind of love, the "Christmas cactus" love, is defined by fortitude and endurance. When you find "Christmas cactus" kind of love, you can withstand a little neglect caused by everyday life struggles and still have enough positive energy to blossom anyway.

There is only one thing which makes the soul of a sentient being complete, and that thing is unconditional love.

" I know I am good 'cause God don't make no junk."

This quote was on a paper taped to the wall at my co-worker's desk. My dear sweet friend Rendy Caldwell, a fellow Child Support Enforcement Agent.

Your mind is not catching it yet, right? Unconditional love from God using bad grammar? Working to catch people who owed money?
True example that life is never a simple act. There are two sides to every story.

Rendy and I were instant friends, from the moment we met.
Never a more loyal and caring person will you meet in my dear Rendy.

As we worked each day, couldn't help to read it repeatedly for years. Isn't it satisfying to believe you are beautiful because you were meant to be, just as you are?

To explain the job of a Support Enforcement Agent, we had the sometimes-impossible task of locating "absent parents". (An absent parent is a biological or legal parent who is not in the child's life for numerous and various reasons. Sometimes it is clearly not the absent parent's fault.)
The task of child support is a task of figuring out what happened. We sometimes gave children a personal history they would have never had any other way.

Daily gleaning of Identifying information from witnesses and governmental or public records grows a case of facts, ultimately allowing children a foundation to build on. A strong foundation with concrete proof of who they really are. This foundation gives them roots. Hopefully, it grounds them so they can begin life with truth and base fabric filled with those who unconditionally love them.

This act of grounding a person can be related directly back to tending to the weave of your fabric. When you are weaving with true knowledge and natural fibers your fabric will grow strong and supple. You will be able to withstand many trials (tugging and friction burns), and still stay together and forging onward.

This work we did affected children profoundly. This work deeply penetrated through the layers and sometimes actual generations of local families.

Rendy went about her tasks very differently than most. Rendy believed in loving everyone, no matter what. She did it without asking if they were worthy.

Everyone was important to her...and most people did rise to the occasion! Good thing too, because our job was not too safe.

We worked out of a basement office in the social services department building, through locked doors and behind bullet proof glass.

We were the ones to push against the human tide and make our cases, so children were properly identified and properly taken care of in life.

Rendy was the kind of person who lived what she preached. She never gave up. She taught me patience; she gave everyone unconditional love.

Rendy showed me true love.
She was taken wickedly by disease at only 39 years old.
Yet her work lives on, deeply impacting generations of children and families. Her short life of only 39 years, gave the world a living legacy. She gave hundreds of children a future and an identity.
Today and every day, I am proud she called me a friend. The last time I ever spoke with her; I ended the call with "I love you!". I am so glad.

Because of this deep love and mutual respect between us, we were able to use our intuition in decision making.

What does intuition mean to you?

Intuition can mean many things, but some basic concepts are: Listen to your heart.
Listen to the Divine Spirit calling from the center of your heart.
Your heart hears only good, wants only to help.

Your heart song is the most important thing you can listen to every day.

The basic notion of a book of thoughts, ideas and blessings began when I, like everyone else, started to notice my body aging, yet was stuck with a young person's mind.
I am not finished living yet!

Any author dreams of resonating with their audience. When I sat down to write, I wanted to share the loves in my life, the blessings in my life, with everyone in the world. So many blessings. So many beautiful moments.
It is not enough to have lived.

My life's motivation has always been to help others. In trying to offer help to others, I have grown and learned. I love the differences in people. It is exciting to learn about new people.

This book is meant as a legacy, so I may touch everyone. Finally, giving the world something to stand the test of time. Something immortal.

To explain immortality is basic. Immortality is created when you bring a creation into existence, which can possibly impact future generations.

This little book is filled with all different concepts/pathways explaining how to reach unconditional love. The people in these stories suffered and triumphed. The people is these stories are real.

Unconditional love is immortal.
Unconditional love is ever-present and lasts through eternity.

The view of my daily human job here on Mother Earth is to endeavor to create safety, comfort, and, hopefully joy, for people.

Don't you think it is a worthy goal in life to give mankind a sense of safety, comfort, joy and especially hope?

In teachings, watching all the "light givers" work is to enjoy being in service to others. My personal work mantra has always been set on, "do as much as possible in the time you have". My goal is to do it as much as possible while I am able.

But alas, I am only mortal. The work I do for the betterment of mankind will someday cease.

What shall I leave to this world in the end?

When I began sharing what I have learned in these pages, my own growth began. Please learn and grow with me. Please open your mind on this journey through these stories and proverbs and thoughts on love.

Just Be, There Is Only One Love.

Do you truly believe in the magic of it all?

Chapter Two
Love of Friendship

FRIENDSHIP IN WINTER

Friendship in Winter

Gaelic tradition teaches each tree has a soul just as humans do. Imagine thinking this cool concept? To believe all life is one life force?

So here, I enjoy thinking friends are like trees. They stand tall and strong. Sometimes alone, sometimes in a group. They support you when you need a whole new life; like a bird building a nest in a branch. If danger approaches, they can just lift you up to a higher level, an upper branch, or make a terrible racket and scare the fear away.
They are there to offer unconditional love. Trees, like friends, are there in the sunrise after the long night, they are there in the twilight, sometimes only to listen and just be silent.

> "I love you in a place
> that there is no space and time, I love you for my life,
> you are a friend of mine"

"A Song for You", Leon Russell

Songwriters offer their friendship to the world through their raw, melodic compositions. Leon Russell is one of the most prolific singer/songwriters in my lifetime. His career lasted four decades and counting. To me, he is as important to the music world as Mozart, Handel, Leonard Cohen, Joni Mitchell or Johnny Cash.

I know that sounds like an odd combination of composers, but each has changed my life with their creations. Can you imagine changing a person's life with your creation? Isn't that an exquisite thought?

This book took a long time to create, and a lot happened during those months. As I write, both Mr. Russell and award-winning composer, Leonard Cohen left our world within days of each other. Heaven must have needed some precious music for a special occasion.

Our modern-day society (1900- 2020+) owes much gratitude to Leon Russell and Leonard Cohen, as they shaped contemporary music with their original creations, then they allowed others to propagate the original work freely in their own style. Other bands recorded their work, lots of people danced to their work. They allowed people to bond over music, and to be happy.

Russell and Cohen's work, their humanly labors, benefitted all mankind.

(February 14, 2015 – I was blessed to see Leon Russell LIVE on stage at Sugar Loaf Performing Arts Center, Sugar Loaf, New York.

It was snowing up a good storm outside. None of the audience cared!

Leon Russell walked out and sat down at the piano, and all the sudden, jaw dropping music emanated from this fragile frame topped with white hair. The audience was silent, rapt. He played 16 songs or so in about 55 minutes: fast and powerful music.

(Privately, before the music started, I handed his attaché behind the stage, a rolled Maternal Nature print from this book, with a note thanking him for his love in my life. The first time I heard him I was 14 and had been jamming ever since, and I told him he made me happy so many times.
I know it was silly, but I sure do hope he got to read my note.)

"A friend is one who knows all about you and loves you anyway."

A friend is someone who loves you unconditionally. A friend does not judge your actions. Friends applaud your strengths and help you with your weaknesses.
They nurture you and make your life better just by caring.

These words are from a calligraphy on a wall-hanging at my mother's house. Her friend of 45 years sent it to her for her birthday.

The words are dedicated to lifelong friends and my mother, who taught me to value
every person who takes time to care for me.

Another deep encompassing thought which balances life in a different way, I found a treasure about living in harmony with all those around you.

You do not need to do anything more than be kind to each other.

**"I want to live by the side of the road
and to be a friend to man."**

(14) A passage from a needlepoint poem, this wall hanging is one of two verses from a poem by Sam Walter Foss. The actual name of the poem is The House by the Side of the Road. The actual words of the poem are "Let me live in a house by the side of the road/And be a friend to man"

I dedicate these lines to my Aunt Melanie, one of Mom's best friends. These words were embroidered on a framed needlepoint, probably from the early 1800's. Aunt Melanie's Mom collected antiques. The needlepoint hung in mother's stone farmhouse.

As we, (her daughter Lorie, my brother, Lorie's first cousins- everybody!) ran through the farmhouse halls as young children, I would pause and read it that passage, over and over again.

"Be a friend to man" made an impression on me then, I was only learning how to be a person. Hopefully, I would like to think that I have lived my life that way. To live to be "a friend to man".

Interestingly, Aunt Melanie is not my real aunt, she is a dear friend to my Mom. I use the title out of respect and love.

You see, in speaking of creating friendships, I believe giving respect allows two things to happen; first you receive it back and second it starts a level of trust. Aunt Melanie experienced every triumph and bruise with my family. Someone who romped and played at the beach with us. Someone who treated me as her family. Who allowed me to enjoy her Mom's incredible farm on the side of a mountain,
where I learned what a good friend should be.

**"Friendship is unnecessary,
like philosophy,
like art...
It has no survival value; rather it is one of those things that
gives value to survival."**

-C.S. Lewis

C.S. Lewis had a powerful idea. His thought was to value people over all else. My wish is society, all of it, would embrace then practice daily, this value, today and every day.

Fraternal bonding leads to an improved quality of life for all. A feeling of connectivity leads to a feeling of safety.

There is strength in numbers.

Promise to a Friend:
Today and every day,
I will fill myself with love and share it with the world.

Promise to the universe: Others may treat me as they will.
Their choices of how they treat me become their karma, their path. How I respond, is mine.

Promise about this thing called, "Life"

The intentions here are very clear. There will be dark and light.
There will be right and wrong. There will be trials and truths.

There will be a path,
and it will be revealed through time and patience,
for the universe moves deliberately and decisively.

Contributions from all my friends: Everyone sent me thoughts! You know, anyone can be your friend with time and patience.

My friends sent ideas about what it means to them to cherish their good friends. May you all find a way to surround yourselves with kind loving friends in your life too.

Friendship is like flowers in full bloom.
(A bit of surprise happiness to make your day a little brighter)

Friendship is when no awkward moments occur.
(When they do, it usually results in hysterical laughter)

True friendship is being there through good and bad times.
(if you have friends for decades you will most certainly have times of both trials and happiness)

The best therapy is just hanging out and doing absolutely nothing with your friend.
(Less is more! concept)

True friendship allows you to be totally candid and truthful with each other.
(Each one of us gets wounded from time to time.)

True friendship is, even after being apart for years, being able to pick up where you left off as if no time had passed. (this is the most exquisite type of unconditional love- it is nurturing and balanced and so comforting)

The other day, I read a good quote likening friendship to trees.
"Be Like a Tree, Both Rooted and Reaching"

Which fits organically in with…

> **"A true friend is one who thinks**
> **you are a good egg,**
> **Even if you are half-cracked…"**

Friendship is funny and warms the heart.

The true meaning of friendship is revealed when nothing matters but the other person.

I implore each of you to take a moment, uncover how another person is faring.

Everyone seems to be fighting daily battles. This journey is arduous. Many people travel extensively to accomplish their daily work. Many hard-working people come home from work weary.

A friend sees the best for you, when you cannot see it for yourself. Use your friends as a mirror to your soul.
They will show you what your heart most desires. They will encourage you to pursue your dreams.

Such important people to have in your life!

Let this be our destiny to love, to live,
to begin each new day together, to share our lives together.

Don't they say this kind of thing at most wedding ceremonies?

One of my sweet friends sent me this. My friend was first a nurse and then became an elementary school teacher.

Complete optimist.
Can you imagine?

My friend learned to be a nurse, then she studied the sciences, then she learned to teach.

She is now a finely tuned public-school teacher
who is quick witted and well-rounded. She loves her job.

The burdens of society are upon our schools.

She puts aside time from
a son, a grandchild, a job, a dog, a cat, a house.
She paused everything to find me a thought or an idea for my book.

She is someone who leaves footprints in my heart with her kind words and gentle encouragement.

Could your child be in better hands? I think not. She makes it look easy.

Can we raise a better generation?
Can we teach our children kindness and respect for Mother Earth and all its inhabitants?

There are many people destined to stay with you for a moment, a short time, a season,
and for a very good reason...
but very few become true friends.

They leave an imprint on you,
your thoughts are warm and glowing with them in mind.

This is the kind of soul I wish for you in your life. A true friend.
One who will coach you,
answer questions without asking why and the ones who will love you
when your hair has turned blue accidently.

This passage is meant to convey what it means to have "true blue"
friends. True blue means they stay with you through thick and thin.

I questioned all my friends about unconditional love.
We all feel the same way. Unconditional love gives life meaning.

> **Walking with a friend in the dark is better
> than walking alone in the light**
>
> *— Helen Keller (12)*

After some research, I found Hellen Keller moved to Forest Hills, Queens, New York City, together with Anne Sullivan Macy and John Macy, her long time and greatly supportive friends. Keller used the house as a base for her work on behalf of the American Foundation for the Blind.
Ms. Keller chose to live with her dear friends the Macy's, and it was a good situation for all involved.
Even though they were not blood, they were family.
Through the safety at the Macy home, Ms. Keller was comfortable enough to take a chance on love.
Once in your life, everyone should take a chance on love.

A significant amount of Hellen Keller's items was in storage in vaults in the World Trade Center when it fell. The world lost many irreplaceable things that day. Let us never forget how fleeting life can be.

Love each other now!

**We are never far apart,
for friendship doesn't count the miles- it is measured by the heart.**

This sentiment needed to be included in a chapter about the love of friends.

After many decades on this Mother Earth, there are many people I do not get to see often, they live far away yet,

they are so valuable in my life.

> **Friends show their love in times of trouble, not in happiness.**
>
> *– Euripides*

I would also add no distance, and no lapse of time will ever lessen the friendship of two persons

who are committed to understanding the worth of each other.

Friends Uplift the Soul During moments of darkness,

any act of kindness can offer consolation. Any soul can make you more comfortable.

True friends help you heal and bring light

back into your heart.

Chapter Three

The Wisdom of Love

BELIEF IN IMMORTAL WISDOM

Belief in Immortal Wisdom

(Sunset over Big Sur, California) original is 14x11, acrylic on canvas

This day was a magical day. Nature has a wisdom all its own. The physical chemistry (some call it alchemy) of life manifests into a shimmering mist of vibrant colors
illuminated by the sun's rays of golden light.
Suddenly, senses become enlivened – the feel of the breeze, the smell of the ocean, and warm gentle sunlight. There is nothing quite like it. You feel transformed into another realm.

The painting creates a sense of wonder, beckoning the acceptance of what is already past, and an optimism for what is yet to come. The future will bring you infinite possibilities for love, light, tranquility, and peace. God is infinite and so are the blessings you will receive; it is all part of the grand plan for this Mother Earth.

Just Be, just love.

Enjoy the journey, into the horizon, into infinity.

**"A loving heart
is the truest wisdom"**

Philosophers may say wisdom comes when you are receptive, and it comes in all kinds of ways. Wisdom usually comes through experience. Creating feelings of Loyalty and Belonging tend to foster a safe environment for learning. Learning creates profound wisdom.

There is wisdom in knowing exactly what
the reality is, and how it fits into your everyday life.

There is wisdom in loving openly and honestly.
There is wisdom in enjoying real relationships, based on trust.
The wisdom grows as you develop a continuous sense of loyalty and belonging.
This can all start by something simple and easy: kindness.

To live with a gentle and kind spirit is our continued goal.
Be ever guided by the desire to promote success and happiness for all.
Please live in your own joy, doing what you love.

The wisdom of love and balance. Love must be balanced. There can be no false dependence on realities which are not simply balanced, or in other words, not realistic.

Both parties must be equal in the awareness of the relationship. Equally desiring the one goal, yet individually set by each person.

A real relationship has real emotion.
Do not enter a relationship unless you want to feel real emotion for someone else.
When those real emotions flow from kindness, everything flows into the development of a sense of love for all.
This is why the feeling of family comes so naturally.

Let us now discuss the wisdom of how you live daily.
Look around.
Do you like what you see?
Ok, now close your eyes and see from the heart.

Do you like what you see?

Please know this is your true essence.

It is the truth of how you have woven your fabric.
The heart can see beauty and love,
more wondrous than the eyes can ever see.

Use your heart to show you the way to wisdom.
There is always another chance to grow.
Just keep trying!

Your journey and your life fabric will become stronger by each trial. Each failure might create a tiny hole in your fabric, but please persevere, for quitters never win! Fabric can always be mended!

How can you succeed in what you abandon? Quitters have quit before they have even tried...

*Love me when I least deserve it, because
that is when I really need it.*

-A Swedish proverb

Life sends you good and bad experiences.

When you see the good and the bad in people, you must make a choice.

If you make a conscious decision and a clear choice to believe in the innate goodness of mankind, you then can love them without feeding into their drama. This, my friends, *is the wisdom in love.*

Your life becomes enlivened and energized because
of kindness which has lead to comfort, safety and finally love. You allow yourself to cultivate great spirit.
You allow yourself to weave strong fibers into your fabric. Even if, sometimes, they are strange colors and wild sizes!

A Miracle
is a shift in perception from fear to love.

Humans and animals have unique survival abilities. Fear is part of the arsenal of survival techniques.

In "The Wisdom of Love" we learn the lesson of knowledge.

It is the knowledge of when to fear and when not to fear, while living in the moment.

Fear and Love

No book on love would be complete without discussing fear of love.

Fear has taught us to stop.

But when we decide to love we also decide
to become excited, open, accepting. This leads to risk, which then leads to passion.

If we live in passion, we are happy and content with life.

Let's use a simple example:

We love our bicycle and can't wait to ride it, but if we fall off
do we quit loving the bike?
No, we get up and try to learn how to ride better, so, we do not fall again.

Then why can't this be true with loving?

So then why can't we forgive ourselves when we try to love and stumble?

My belief? We only stumble in love because that person had a specific time and place to be with us.

Next time, we can learn to love a little differently, a little better.

If you surround yourself with like-minded people or simply encircle yourself with kind people,
it will most likely lead to love in your life.

When we face the future with
courage and an open heart, we then can embrace life and truly provide positive interactions.

Evolution comes to all, whether we are prepared or not. Wisdom in loving allows the eventual hope for a better world.

To be alive, acting fearlessness and open-hearted, Is the vision of people who embrace life.

Mastering this concept is to become fearless in love.

There are many sides, also called aspects, to love. The secret is to love openly and then forgive others who cannot love back. The secret seems to be to always believe deeply in romance, but only give your heart to someone who has the capability to give their heart to you as well. Someone who can love you back. Someone who can love your heart as your heart needs. To know when someone can give you your unique kind of romance.

Please try to persevere in kindness. Even if does not result in love.
Please, just try to be someone who brightens days and shares words of encouragement.

Please believe change will come when you are trying.

Some positive ways to help others is to believe them when they have a hunch, it will give them confidence. And to hug someone when they fail, kind ways always lead to a positive change.

Try to surround yourself with friends who love unconditionally.

Weave friends into your fabric of life who are loyal. Life would be much less without friends. Their loyalty becomes so comforting.

Some of us started out as our parent's best friends' kids or classmates in elementary school and eventually cheerleaders in junior high school who kept up cheering for people our whole lives.

A strong fabric of friendships represents everything good and strong and faithful.

Long woven with experience and hard work created a life fabric filled with wise, true friends. Thick, strong threads of colorful memories.
We all add love to everything we do.
We need more people like us on this Mother Earth.

The wisdom of love can be found in practice. You must practice loving, since there is good and evil on this Mother Earth and we want to make sure we always attract good, with good behaviors, whether it be for yourself or for someone else.

The beauty of cultivating good loving behavior is behavior can be learned, and if necessary, modified.

In other words, there is always hope, you can bring more love into your life.

Here are 10 easy steps leading to more love in your life. (HA! They are arduous!) But so, equally rewarding to master. May you be blessed with this change to your behavior. (I am probably still working on some of them)

10 WAYS TO LOVE

1. Listen intently and with compassion
2. Speak, knowing words are powerful
3. I Answer, using kindness
4. Share, withholding nothing
5. Enjoy every waking moment and those of sleep, too
6. Trust, giving it and expecting it
7. Forgive, with gratitude for the lessons
8. Promise without forgetting
9. Give without sparing
10. Pray without ceasing

The wisdom of love includes this thought too:

You can love more than one person at the same time, different people fulfill different needs,
and for that...you love them.

This concept was sent to me by my childhood friend, another of my elementary schoolmates, my friend for life. I always tell her that we learned how to be people together. We learned how to love unconditionally and how to be grateful.

Please believe there is a full spectrum of love,
from innocence to betrayal, from first contact to last goodbye. This is where the fear of love comes from.
Universal law states there is always a balance required to every action:
With every powerful action
There will be a balanced response.

To share the wisdom of unconditional love with more than one person at one time is to show love in every action – holding a door for someone, making sure someone with a broken leg has a seat on the bus. These are all acts of wisdom in love. To promote peace and prosperity for all allows your own life to prosper. This wisdom allows you to find and enjoy a sense of true love.

True love is the balance between anxiety and satiety.

Heavy concept, right?

Try to start here…
True love is total balance.
In balance, there is no need. True love is complete. No need to anticipate. No need for desire.
It is perfect and unconditional.

Think of true love as a very ornate but sturdy thread. You deeply weave that person into your fibers.

With each jubilant experience, their brightly colored fibers make beautiful patterns in your fabric. Each of your threads begin to fill the necessary holes and enhance your own life fabric. Creating beauty and stability in your life.

The wisdom of love teaches us to express gratitude. The formula is quite simple:

    Inhale Love…
    …Exhale Gratitude

And repeat as many times as necessary.

Please find any little thing to be grateful for. Examples of things to be grateful for are: Comfortable shoes! Petting a furry animal. Watching a child play by themselves, or simply sleep quietly. Waking up to sunshine.

Every day, we have another chance to create.

Every night, we have another chance to resolve our day, cleanse our spirit of the day's residue.
Every moment, we have the chance to love and remember we can be incredibly grateful.

Please learn to live this way. It is so easy! I promise.

Try to keep in mind, it is an honor to live when others didn't get the chance.

Threads from my fabric were taken too soon. It is always important to keep adorning yourself with joyous loving people. That way, if someone's destiny is to leave, you can fill the hole they leave. It is not always their fault they had to leave, but it is your responsibility to weave your own life fabric.

Here are more thoughts on the wisdom of love. Living in a true real sense can be fruitful. The wisdom in love teaches us to:

Be present.
Buy a plant and nurture it, water it. Walk, run, keep moving.
Create art, any type of art- paint, sculpt, knit, craft, jewelry. Just create.
Swim in the ocean or swim in a lake. Bring an umbrella and walk in the rain. Take chances. Do not be afraid to fail.
Love others as you want them to love you.
Avoid small talk yet learn to embrace conversation. Ask questions. Make mistakes.
But learn from those mistakes. Learn everything you can! Know your worth. You are worth it.
Love fiercely. Forgive quickly. Let go of the old.
Old thoughts, old ways- let them go.
Keep only what serves your best interests.
Promise yourself to keep only what makes you happy. This formula promises to lead to love every day.

My Dad always says, **"Everything you do should make you money or make you happy. If it does not make you money, or it does not make you happy. Do not do it!"** (This theory helps to learn good boundaries and behaviors.)

The wisdom in love is shown here in a different way.

> **What you expect is defined by the mind,**
> **Whereas**
> **the heart explores your unlimited potential.**
>
> *-Harold W. Becker, #thelovefoundation (5)*

Found this simple, yet wise quote and thought immediately of my hopelessly and endlessly romantic cousin.
She believes these things to be true: Love always finds a way.
Kindness helps every situation. Loyalty is an expression of love;
for when she gives her heart, she gives it all.

We cannot speak of wisdom without a mention of success. To know unconditional love is to have the greatest success.

Success:
cannot be accurately measured by money or status. Its measure is...
love.

There can be no complete discussion of love and success without the mentioning of fear.

Fear is natural.
Fear is a biological response and it works effectively as a survival skill.

If you venture into love, go whole-heartedly. What if you genuinely succeed?

The possibilities for success are as infinite as love itself.

Reading these words teaches you to learn what is meant by the simple concept of success in love.

Really, love, success in love, can be very simple, if you allow it to be.

Chapter Four
Love Never Fails

Golden Ephemeral Love

Love Never Fails
This is a simple view looking south, down the California coastline at the Pacific Ocean. God gave us Mother Earth who shares her beauty with each of us. The golden, majestic, and vibrant colors are for all to see. Love will never fail you; it is not able. Love is for everyone. It is of no consequence who you are, or how you arrived there, if you are looking at the sunset in this painting you are receiving the love of the universe, it is your gift.

Author's Note:

As I stood overlooking the Pacific Ocean at Big Sur, California, I thought to paint the view I saw, so I took this photograph. After I reproduced it on canvas, I chose the vista for the Wisdom of Love. It beckons a vision into the future, into the horizon, and into infinity.

Big Sur is a naturally extraordinary, awe-inspiring place. The colors from the ocean shimmer through mist and golden rays of refracted light. You feel swept into a gentle, yet vital surge of energy, creating an enlivening of your senses. Go ahead, take some time. Smell the ocean, bask in the rays of the sun and indulge in the natural hot springs, all is yours to experience.

Dream, with a sense of wonder, and profound knowing of what has come to pass.

Heal and reconcile that past and hope for what is yet to come.

In this chapter we will explore life, hope, faith, trust .
"Love Never Fails", think of these words. What do these words mean to you?
Love will never fail.
Never fail?

Let us break these words down. Love never-
-Never fail

Recognize this? *If you never love, you will never fail at love.*

But will you have truly lived if you have lived without love?

Love will never fail because love is an unconditional universal force provided through our chemistry into our minds. We cannot shield ourselves from love's universal effects, it could unite the world!

Conversely, the lesson in an individual one. A good one. A simple one.

Blend kindness into every action and carefully weave a fabric of compassionate and loving people around you.

Weave your fabric of life well. Find success in your careful attention to living in a loving state. Living in a loving environment.

Recognize this one next? *If you love more, you will never fail!*

Let us start a discussion with exploring a perspective from another religion. The Quran is the holy book of the Islamic faith.

> **"Love does not need to be perfect. it just needs to be true."**
>
> *-The Quran*

I believe this to be true. Love will not fail, if it is true. Unconditional love is resilient.

This is decidedly not a religious discussion, but I want a person who believes In true love around me. Regardless of how they achieve unconditional love.

My deep belief is unconditional love is God's love in the universe.

God's unconditional love pervades every fiber, every molecule of our existence; deep into the earth, trees, animals, humans. Through every generation, without fail, all have derived strength from love.

As this chapter explores the concept of "love never fails" there were lots of different aspects to write about.
Religious? Spiritual? Organic? Tribal? Physiological?
(The animal kingdom has many stories of the males and females bonding for life- there is an evolutionary and very physical reason for the success of bonding.)

I had many discussions with close friends and family.
My childhood girlfriend and I discussed what it meant to be unconditionally loved. She sent me these thoughts after our discussion, and I added my own thoughts beneath them.

"Love is magical, and it gives you strength to transform your pain."

Any pain. It can be physical or emotional. To know you are loved makes life's daily grind and everyday troubles much more bearable.

"True love is like a stone anchoring you through choppy waters."

We are taught to believe that love will never fail us. A safety net in a storm.

This will always be true if we give of ourselves properly and freely. We must also then remember to receive love equally well.

This is a lovely passage which will take 2 seconds to read and a long time to understand. That is just as well. It becomes a powerful tool in time.

> **Whenever we can manage to love**
> **without expectations, calculations, negotiations, we are**
> **indeed in heaven.**
>
> *– Rumi*

We have a whole lifetime to perfect this skill! Love never fails.

Hopefully, we will learn the value of each interaction
early in life and evolve to reach heaven on this Mother Earth. Have comfort in the wisdom of love.
Have the courage to pour incredible loving kindness into any project, and the project will immediately propel itself into being.

Love enough to cause a creation.

Any creation will do. A refurbished chair? A book? A painting? A child?

This is a story about a man I met through my "day job" where I go around to appointments in people's homes. This man and I came from two completely different walks of life- different ages, different parts of the country, different work, different lifestyles, yet we immediately became fast friends.

He grew up in Texas and I grew up in New York. We joke about having totally different speech patterns while still speaking English!

As I learned about him, he showed me quickly he was a wonderful person. All our "supposed differences" meant nothing, because we spoke to each other in kindness and showed each other great respect.

One day, I told him I was writing a book on 10 ways to reach unconditional love. He smiled as he rose out of his chair and went to the other room to a bureau and dug out a beat-up old notebook. The tattered and stuffed notebook was packed full of well-worn pages of things he has been inspired to write. He had poured much emotion into those well-worn pages, let me tell you! His writings are an expression of his deep soul and compassionate heart. The passage belongs in Love Never Fails because it is true.

He wrote the piece below as a tribute to the untimely death of Princess Diana. It is written in his East Texas style of speech, untouched by me.

Our universal love for Princess Diana is unconditional. The 1980's were my youth; I was soaking up knowledge like a sponge. In world events, the British royal family was growing. Princess Diana married the Queen's son and set to work as an Ambassador for her country.

Princess Diana defined a generation of beneficent caring.

It seemed, everyone on the planet knew of her exuberance for life and her incredible spirit. She embodied universal love. She devoted herself to useful work and critical projects for everyone on Mother Earth. Princess Diana was concerned with everyone on this planet. My friend genuinely believes Princess Diana demonstrated to humanity the simple and true concept of love never fails.

"She rose from the depths of an invisible mist with the beauty and grace from the mighty hands of God
With that for all, everything and everyone she touched would rise and follow her to the end
She had looks of a gentle sunset that would take the hearts and still away all the hurt and hate. To form a rainbow of beauty and love that seemed to stay forever and a day. She had something beyond her own knowledge, something that no mankind could ever take away. To be such a small figure of a lady; she had more than any of our great ones that ever was or were to come. It was beyond our imagination of what it was. For someone so small, she stood tall. She was as wide as our mighty oceans or seas, she stood tall as our tallest trees. She was more beautiful than our great land, with landscapes of rose gardens. She had more love than you could dream in a hundred lifetimes. No matter how much, large or small, she gave with love.
She gave with grace, she gave with charm, she gave with beauty, and she gave with style. But most of all, she gave with a smile. It was a smile that will live on in our hearts for times to come one thing is for sure. They will know and for they may say, she lives within us forever and a day. For those of us have heart and take heart, may ask what is life? And what is death?
For now, our invisible mist is gone away to rest."

Love Never Fails includes belief in God, and the faith in his plan. This chapter is a plea. A plea for everyone to have faith and hope at their darkest hour. When things just do not make sense. Trust in love.

Let us now turn to celebrate wisdom, friendship and deep bonds, even as nothing else makes sense.

The following are two stories of normal, healthy, vital and beautiful women whose lives were cut short by fate. Yet, they remain alive today in the infinite love their hearts bestowed on those closest to them.

Please know, you will be remembered by those you loved. To have loved, is to have lived.

The first story came during the time I was writing. HN Books, our publishing company was creating many projects and each creation was being completed by many deeply respected subcontractors. Tony is one of the best. We work as a finely tuned instrument as we create fiction and inspiration. Life's work can be love in itself.

The following words are dedicated to his sister, Caroline.

Mr. Neil Diamond sings:

"Sweet Caroline (Good Times Never Seemed So Good)". 1969

"Where it began I can't begin to knowing But then I know it's growing strong Was in the spring And spring became a summer Who'd believe you'd come along Hands Touching handsReaching out Touching me Touching you	One Touching oneReaching out Touching me Touching you Sweet Caroline Good times never seemed so good I've been inclined To believe they never wouldOh no no
Sweet Caroline Good times never seemed so good I've been inclined To believe they never wouldBut now I Look at the night And it don't seem so lonely We fill it up with only two And when I hurt Hurting runs off my shoulders How can I hurt when holding you?	Sweet Caroline Good times never seemed so goodSweet Caroline I believe they never couldSweet Caroline

Caroline, a perfectly healthy mother of an older daughter and younger twin girls, got in her car and started her way to work. In an instant, she sustained catastrophic head trauma in a car accident. Adding to the pain, Tony and Caroline's beloved Mother succumbed to a long-term illness only eight months before her daughter's accident.

We say now, twin souls tend to fly together.

There tends to be evidence there are angelic beings here on Mother Earth. Senseless reality handed to us in an unplanned, inexplicable moment. Faith our only solace. The only thing I am sure about on this Mother Earth, is unconditional love leads us back to God. I am sure they are with our Lord.

Caroline then embodied the notion of "love conquers all" as she then saved many other people by donating her organs. Her children have a hero. Hopefully, remembering Caroline here will bring a little bit of peace to everyone who loved her. Please help loved ones to remember ones they have lost. It gives them glimpses of unconditional love from the universe. To me, energy is never extinguished, only changed into different matter.
There are no worldly answers as to why and when you are called home. As these pages unfolded into this love-filled creation, Tony was there to help me, without thinking to ask why or to question my motives. He just helped unconditionally. He has my profound gratitude.

The only truth to be sure of, is unconditional love.

The second story was envisioned by my old college friend, as we were reminiscing . When Lisa heard the call for thoughts of unconditional love, she suggested passages from the Christian Bible, possibly as a tribute to her sister Chris. She wanted to capture the legacy of love Chris left us all. Chris was taken wickedly from this Mother Earth, husband, and children at only 31 years old, leaving two toddlers and newborn twins.

When this happened to Chris, it happened to us all. We were all too young for this kind of thing to happen. The news was surreal. The reality was unfathomable. We had completed our studies and had just begun careers.

How could this happen? Life had just started!

Chris was called home because of fast moving, aggressive cancer. After she was diagnosed and had thoroughly discussed her options for treatment, she stoically decided her own fate. Chris had to choose between the twins she was carrying or her own life.

It was one or the other.

We do not know the reasons for fate.

We must love all we can, as well as we can. That is the only truth.

Chris knew this.

She made her decisions with a pure heart.

She is everything brave and strong, and she lived in and then left this world full of faith and goodness for all.

When writing a book on love it is important to discuss those beautiful souls who did not make it to old age.

My friend Lisa and I have been friends since college, when we were learning how to be adult people, career people. She chose a very rewarding career. She has turned her life into something more. Lisa has experienced the miracle of birth as an Obstetrics Nurse and Midwife for over 30 years now.

Lisa wrote:
"Seventeen years ago, I spent the day surrounded by love, family and friends, helping my sister
to make her transition out of her earthly body.
It was one of the hardest days and at the same time, most beautiful. Beautiful because her strength, dignity and love filled us all.
Those who were there were forever changed by that day. I love her and miss her more than I could ever say.
The pain of living without her ebbs and flows, but never goes away. For those of you who are reading this,
take her message of love. Live every day.
Don't sweat the small stuff.
Make peace and realize how wonderful life is. Appreciate how life is with your siblings.
No one can take the place of my sister who grew to be my best friend. Hug your sisters today, or at least reach out to them.
Send our family love and prayers, if you pray."

Lisa wrote to me about her sister Chris, and we sent a group message out, so Chris's four children and friends from her youth were able to respond.

I was so happy to be able to capture these memories here.
God Bless Chris's beautiful children!
(They are grown now and well on their life's journey. I get to see their pictures and cheer for them vicariously.)

Everyone was given a little piece of Chris's love the day we all shared these memories.
Please remember, love will never fail you. Love conquers all.

After a pretty good debate, (quite a few passages in the Bible about love), Lisa suggested a specific quote as an answer to the overwhelming questioning conjured by saying the words, "love never fails".

Then more questioning led me in another direction
and I found Rumi's quote on belonging to only the religion of love. Both are valid to me if love leads you to God.

> *Love.*
> *It always protects, always trusts, always hopes, and always perseveres. Love never fails.*
>
> — From the King James Bible, 1 Corinthians 13:7-8.
>
> *I belong to no religion. My religion is love.*
> *Every heart is my temple.*
>
> — *Rumi*

Both quotes convey the same message. They are both correct. The human body needs unconditional love. Everyone is entitled to unconditional love, no matter how they get there.

Just Be, There Is Only One Love...

This passage is dedicated to Caroline and Chris:

"Love is patient and kind:
love does not envy or boast; it is not arrogant or rude.
It does not insist on its own way; it is not irritable or resentful;
it does not rejoice at wrongdoing, but rejoices in the truth.
Love bears all things,
believes all things, hopes all things, endures all things.
Love never fails.
So now faith, hope and love abide,
these three; but the greatest of these is love."
King James Bible, 1 Corinthians 13:4-8, 13

When I asked Lisa for permission to share such a painful life event in a book, she replied, "That would be perfect, Colleen. Those words came straight from my heart, before I even woke up, after getting a message from my niece (who is in Taiwan) about a dream she had of her mom. Also, read comments and take what others have said.

Thanks Colleen."

You see, it seems as I was putting this work together,

Lisa posted a picture of her sister on social media on the 17th anniversary

of her passing from her earthly body.

The picture was of her sister Chris holding one of her four children. The specific picture was always on permanent display in Lisa's family living room. It was a favorite.

At the time of Chris's death, Chris had two girls and newborn twins-boy and girl. Lisa had a boy and girl, and after Chris left us, Lisa had another little girl.

As a result, my friend Lisa ended up helping to raise a total of seven children with her brother-in-law and loving husband.
Now this gives a new meaning to a marriage. To a loving family!

In doing this little exercise of remembrance, Lisa and I were able to teach a little family history and share a little more of her sister with her children. Here are the responses they posted.

Samantha (Chris's daughter),
"That's funny, I always thought it was my birthday? I didn't realize I had stolen the crown from the birthday girl (sister Victoria). I love this picture of Mom, too. She looks so beautiful."

Lisa (Chris's sister),
"Yes, Sam, you wanted to be the birthday princess!"

Kelly (Chris's friend),
"I actually took this picture and then I remember Andrew (Lisa's son) took my camera and took random pictures of everything lol!! Beautiful picture !!"

Lisa (Chris's sister),
"Really, Kelly? Good work. I have this picture in my living room. You really captured her and there are so few pictures of her."

Debbie (Chris's friend),
"Love this picture and she is wearing the pearls that she lent me for my wedding for something borrowed. Miss her every day".

Here is an example of "love never fails", this time as an example of romantic love.

Let me love you,
if not for the rest of your life, then for the rest of mine.

— Kaceem Madridista (13)

If you love, love completely, cherish the love completely, speak of your love, but most importantly, show your love. Life is finite and fragile. Just because something is there one day, does not mean it will be there the next day. Never take "this moment now" for granted.

Say too much, love too much. Everything is temporary but love.

Love endures, love perseveres, Love is eternal and offers immortality.

Other creatures can provide humans with a love
that will never fail.
People love others, not for who they are, but for how they make them feel.

And animals love us
for how we make them feel and a million other reasons.

Intimacy is not purely physical.
It is an act connecting you so deeply with someone, you feel like you can see into their soul.

Animals have the unique ability to "see" people
much more easily than people do.

Animals are ever mindful and present. Their joy is to serve with faithfulness, to become a strength, a force of love. Their only motivation is to be in love.

Love never fails also includes love of humanity.

"Love is seeing a smile on your face… even when it hurts"

This comes from my dear, sweet friend, who, I suspect, has a different definition of this thought than most of us would.

Some may think it means "smile through your tears"? But this is not what she means here, not a chance.
To her, it means smile always, no matter what, because you are in love with this world.

You see, her job is dealing with the public.
She sees every kind of person and all their individual behaviors,
their life's gains and losses,
tantrums, antics, and sometimes pranks. She is loving and kind and gracious to all.

If you are lucky enough to be called her friend, then you are fully enveloped in unconditional love and many hysterical conversations!

Laughing all the way we will be…

All of life is a journey, a ride, hopefully an adventure. The trick is to find someone who wants to take the ride with you- a friend or a soulmate will do...

"Love doesn't make the world go 'round.
Love is what
makes the ride worthwhile."

And

"Once in a while, right in the middle of an ordinary life, love gives us a fairy tale".

The like-mindedness of these two passages are long etched in time and sentiment.

These words were suggested by my friend today, who was also my next-door neighbor all through our childhood.

She was at least 5 years older than most of us, we all watched and tried to emulate her, after all, she was first to experience everything life had to offer. All of us kids ran all over the street playing and riding bikes. She was in high school and we hid behind a hill watching her smooch a boy! None of us had kissed a boy before. Oh, how we giggled!
She first became a teacher, then a mother, and now a grandmother! Oh my, how time flies when you are having fun.

Very creative person to know.
She is true and kind and everything good. I am lucky to have her in my life.

She has been successfully married for at least three decades and probably a couple years past the third decade.
I think she might be on to something with this one!

"Love never fails" from a man's point of view:

> **"When a man falls in love with a woman, she becomes his weakness.**
> **When a woman falls for a man, he becomes her strength.**
> **Exchange of power."**

This thought was sent by the most romantic and subsequently, well-loved man I know:
another elementary school friend who went through every grade with me since we were five years old.
I think I can now safely say I am sure he is my friend for life.

He served this great country called America when the perils of war struck, and he survived to become a family man, and a good one at that.

To all he meets, his kindness is evident. He lends a hand; he lends an ear; he lends his heart. He is a supporter and a provider and everything good.

Contemplating the concept of "Love never fails" can and may teaches us many things:

Deep loving feeling gives you strength.
Believing in someone
while deeply loving them also gives you courage.

If you have the strength to persevere and if you have the courage to try, you then can also have the courage to laugh at yourself.

If you make a mistake, acknowledge the lesson and move on. Give yourself the benefit of trying.

Give yourself the benefit of listening to your heart Give yourself the benefit of trying and listening without anxiety or strain.
Please allow yourself to relax and love deeper and with more joy.

Just Be, There is Only One Love.

"Love never fails" includes allowing you to dream:

Keep some room in your heart for the unimaginable!

Everything we love, now familiar and comforting, was once new. We lived the excitement and wondrous joy of a new experience and then learned to love over time.

Everything evolves through time and with patience. Imagine what is possible?
When you apply patience and perseverance to positive endeavors, anything becomes possible.

Chapter Five

Love of Self

The Future, Sails Up!

The Future, Sails-Up!

Influenced by the Impressionists, I created a sailboat at anchor, sails are furled, it awaits patiently for instruction. Once the supplies are loaded, you can check the wind and get underway.

Create an adventure to wherever you want to go and stay for however long you wish. Set the navigation to approach your destiny. Find your bliss. Every day is a new chance to try.

Have faith. There is always a future. Every day is a gift. This is your Life. It is, The Future, Sails Up!

This chapter is going to help create ideas about how to learn to love yourself unconditionally.

Let us start from a basic point of view, a mantra of love.

Please say this over and over
until it becomes easy to remember.

It will then help you love yourself more. Just one little step. Start here.

"I am lovable." "I am loving." "I am loved."

Here is a thought for you to contemplate:
Most philosophers say we attract what we are. If you want to love, give love. If you cannot give love, then at least allow yourself to receive love. You will find love comes to you from everywhere.

**The truly rich person
is the one who is in contact with the energy of love
every second of his existence.**
Paulo Coelho, Author

The love you may conjure for yourself can only pale in comparison
to the love you may conjure
when you finally meet the right person.

Take your time and find out who you are before you involve anyone else.

You deserve to wait for something magical!

Here is another path to loving yourself.
Can you learn to love yourself this way? Hopefully you can. It is worth the effort. Truth is the path to unconditional love.

The only way to feel truly loved is to allow your true self to be seen, heard, known, then loved.

*If you conjure and display a totally positive attitude,
living as your authentic self,
the right people can then grow to love the real you.*

This series of thoughts reminds me of the one long continuous conversation between me and my girlie friend every day.

The two of us met at the roller-skating rink and both had big mouths full of braces. We have known each other so long she speaks to me in what we call our "Authentic Self's".

The "Self's" can do anything!

With a wing and a lot of prayers.

To love a friend is to love yourself. Be a friend, who hears a tone of voice and sets off into a fit of hysterical laughter because we know each other so intimately, we know how we stumble...or the time one of us threw their shoes off to dance in a club and one got stolen! And thank God my friend does not drink. Try using only one 3-inch heel to get home. HA! That did not happen. Instead, I had a pair of flip flops in the car.
Not to say chaos ensued but the guys drank alcohol out of the remaining shoe as a requiem to a favorite pair. Good times. We have at times, laughed until it hurt when we give in and everything becomes funny. Tears-down-our-face-funny.

The world becomes possible. Every opportunity, every beautiful day, and every loving animal we enjoy…. We continue to do the hard work to make all our lives the best possible.
(and boy, there are a lot of pets. Between us right now, there are 6 cats, 2 dogs and about 10 fish)

Everything becomes possible if we work at it.

We cheer each other- sometimes it is cheering to spur each other on, sometimes it is cheering to stop each other from doing anything else stupid!

We secretly pray for each other or sometimes we pray straight out loud.

But the best part is, we do not explain anything. We just accept each other, just as we are.
Love yourself. What does love yourself mean to you? Try just doing it. Love yourself as you would another.

The truth is delightfully simple.

Being in love with the person you are, and thinking joyful, happy thoughts are the quickest ways to create
a wonderful life.

Again, the truth is simple. Make your own happiness.

I will call someone to tell them a joke,
or I will call someone to tell them I finally found my car keys. They were in the refrigerator!

Creating fun times can never be wrong if fun is with a kind spirit (Fun might occasionally be inappropriate in our serious world, so play with caution.)

But play!
Remember to play.

Fun is fun.... It will keep you young!

Take another look at an aspect of loving yourself. You are made of Mother Earth; you are made of God. The universal unconditional love.

Here is solid and time-tested knowledge. History handed down through the generations, in the most loving ways. Native Americans enjoy a beautiful freedom of spirit in nature and their own bodies.

This is the unconditional "Love of Self" in action. Wisdom from the Lakota Nation:
"Wakan Tanka, Great Mystery,
Teach me how to trust my heart,
my mind, my intuition,
my inner knowing,
the senses of my body, the blessings of my spirit.
Teach me to trust these things
so that I may enter my sacred space and love beyond fear,
and thus, walk in balance
with the passing of each glorious sun."

This was influenced by my love of my Native American friend,
who is beloved by the bond of the little family we have grown over the past 30 years.

My loving friend, known to us as Magzilla, a most powerful spirit of good.

With each person you fold into your fabric of family and friends, please try to choose strong, balanced, natural and malleable threads.

When you choose what threads to weave deeply into your fabric, weave each unique thread with the intent to make it a strong fabric, but do not hesitate to bring in all kinds of different threads.
Magzilla is my deepest crimson thread (from my heart chakra). We have been friends since the 1980's. She is a beautician, so our joke is, we have as many memories, as we have had hairstyles.
Every phase of our lives has come with joys and crisis. We have been together through them all. After our nascent family was established

when she married her soulmate, then Magzilla and Jeff brought us a son and then another one. This fine soul Magzilla, who illuminated my world, then created more illuminated children to us watch over. One of her children is very musical. It is great fun. I believe to play music is to pray twice because it releases the love in your soul. We all have special gifts to offer this world.

Therefore, my belief is, it is important to adorn your fabric with different and unusual threads.

Now we expand our unconditional love to our loved ones as well. We cheer them all on!

As generations grow, we create more unconditional love and we create a deeper bond, a more spiritual bond.

Blessed beyond belief, tis me! Tis thee.

If you are looking into loving yourself then maybe, just maybe, we should look at what the "self-help" experts have to say.
You can call them gurus, if you wish.
A guru is someone whose life is dedicated to discipline and training. What would be better discipline and training than to fall deeply in love with your own self?

*   *   *

Who knew? What a challenge I set up when I asked for ideas for the Love of Self chapter! My male college buddy sent me this from a self- help guru.

This guru challenged us to understand this idea:

"Love, is to recognize yourself in another..."

Then I responded to my college buddy, asking him what this "reflection" meant to him. I was buzzing with an opinion! And I was curious.

Curious about what the person I admired had to say. I was curious about how another person I respected felt.

With clear thought on an opinion, I do not believe I need to recognize myself in anyone.

In my mind, I am whole and alive and vibrant on my own.
If I chose to become a partner of someone, they must be whole, too.

Then I began to question my thoughts. The conversation in my head went something like this; "Hey, this guy has been successfully married for 24 years. He must know something!"

HA! Foiled again!

This is what he wrote back to me:

"I am not sure.
Maybe it's about how we share a collective consciousness, and you recognize that you
resonate more with one person than any other?"

In Love of Self as our topic, my response is another question. My response is this:
" Maybe you find the right one when you both begin to vibrate at the same frequency,
as other may change your frequency, a partner would only strengthen it."

We are all here to assist each other, I will leave this for my readers to contemplate.

We are all here to help each other find our own way.

Love of self sends best wishes to yourself. Use these words to remind yourself to count every blessing, every minute is a gift.

May you always have:

Beauty for your eyes to see, Sunsets to warm your heart, Rainbows to follow the clouds, Smiles when sadness intrudes, Laughter to kiss your lips, Hugs when spirits sag, Comfort on difficult days, Faith so you can believe, Confidence for when you doubt, Patience to accept the truth, Courage to know yourself, Love to complete your life.

I sent this thought to my childhood friend, who was going through some tough times because of an addiction.

*"As you learn to become in love with yourself, you can change reality.
You can make sure to see the good you do always outweigh the evil you are presently battling.
You can always share a smile or a kindness."*

I wanted him to feel he was still worthwhile and valuable as a person, even though the addiction was babbling senselessly but incessantly in his head.

I wanted to help him, but no one could. He had to learn to first help himself.

Love of self – Who are you?

The next week, I sent the same friend another letter. As encouragement, I added this quote as part of the letter. Later, he told me he hung the letter on the wall next to his bed so every night and every morning he could remind himself of his duty to himself.

Before befriending others,
you have to be your own friend. Before correcting others,
you have to correct yourself. Before making others happy,
you have to make yourself happy.
It's not called selfishness,
it's called personal development.
Once you balance yourself, only then can you
balance the world around you.
(7)

Love of self teaches us patience and generosity.

Unconditional love for yourself does not include vanity or greed. Unconditional love balances satiety and need.

When my friend was asked how he was progressing after rehab, he was upbeat and ready to move forward. It was he who decided to add something to this book for his children.

His unconditional love for the four of them is profound and precisely the place where he nurtured the great strength, he needs every day to get through to the other side of an addiction.

I challenged him; "Ok, you tell me about them all the time, but you never write anything to them. I challenge you to put your feelings into words".

Love of Self meets the Greatest Love

My friend did not need time, wrote back in maybe four seconds flat. It was easy for him.

My love for my children will always be unconditional! In my eyes, they can do no wrong.
It is not a choice I make.
It is something in my heart.
I guess that is why they call me Dad!

You see, no matter what storms and struggles are bearing down on them, parents mostly live and breathe for the well-being of their children.

This may not be true for every child, so I will add this thought:

Every parent gives their child a first thread to weave, whether they stay in the child's life or not. The rest of the fabric is left to be woven by the child's own instinct and willpower.

This quote comes from "A Return To Love"
1992 by Marianne Williamson
but it is commonly mis-attributed to Nelson Mandela, who was said to want to use it as part is his inaugural speech as President of South Africa.

Ms. Williamson has my deepest gratitude for all her work. She is one I lovingly call our self-help guru's. This is one of my favorite passages for inspiration. It gives me hope, it gives me esteem for myself.
Let us now visit with another history making icon of our lifetime.

If you lived under a rock for the last 40 years, you probably would still have heard of Nelson Mandela. He overcame years of imprisonment to triumph by becoming the President of South Africa. He started a struggle for justice and independence. He suffered in jail because of his rebellion but ended up free and becoming President of the very nation which took his freedoms.

If Mr. Mandela did not quit, then I think just maybe you might try just a little harder every day.

Remember in loving yourself, you can achieve what you were put on Mother Earth to do, no matter how hard the tasks to get there.

It will be worth it, I promise.

"Our deepest fear is not that we are inadequate. Our deepest fear is that we are powerful beyond measure.

It is our light, not our darkness that most frightens us.
We ask ourselves, Who am I to be brilliant, gorgeous, talented, fabulous?

Actually, who are you not to be? You are a child of God. Your playing small does not serve the world.
There is nothing enlightened about shrinking so that other people won't feel insecure around you.
We are all meant to shine, as children do.
We were born to make manifest the glory of God that is within us. It's not just in some of us; it's in everyone.
And as we let our own light shine, we unconsciously give other people permission to do the same.
As we are liberated from our own fear, our presence automatically liberates others."

Love of self-shows us how to gracefully accept change.
Whether you fight, kicking and screaming; or whether you accept it, change is going to happen.

My philosophy is consistent, one must adapt quickly and grow into each new reality with grace and dignity. This is a planet of free will.

God loves you and will help you in whatever you ask him to, but he will not interfere with your actions. You own them and their consequences and blessings. God knows all, His will is the universal force which guides us to immortality.

Believe you are worthy of taking a trip and you will go on a journey.
Only on a journey can you find
if you were worthy of taking the trip.

Love of Self teaches us to have patience with our own needs, as well. One recipe for happiness and contentment is as follows:

RECIPE FOR HAPPINESS
(Caution: may also lead to extreme contentment)

First take a nice, long walk.
Find someone to speak about theories and dreams, not people or things.
Debate your opinions. Question your assumptions.
Love yourself for trying so hard every day.

Pay special attention to the moment. Be a little crazy and add love to taste.
Count your minutes and then your blessings.

Let go for a little while and
Just Be

In Love of self it is fair to learn. Learn to create and use your boundaries.

You have every right to:
Stop, Debate, Discuss, Speed up, Slow down
Watch beauty, be beautiful, see beauty Walk slowly, walk fast, skip
Feel the sun on your face
Feel the wind, smell the wind, enjoy the wind You have every right to: be

My favorite thought:
Just Be

I still have a big sky-blue button with a picture of a dove that says, Just Be.

In high school I pinned it to my curtain. Every day, it said Just Be. I read it repeatedly for months and months. Saying those words to myself, allowing myself not to freak out from the vibration buzzing in my brain about the decisions, questions, lessons, interactions…. life…

Just Be…you will get through it…

Love of self teaches the importance of patience.

"Patience is the executioner of worry; the revealer of truth; the lens to discover depth and beauty; the hallmark of consciousness; the demonstration of hope and the soul of love. "(8)

Love of self must demonstrate unconditional love, kindness and compassion.

My other friend named Colleen's big brother sent this pronouncement by Oscar Wilde.

My friend Colleen and I went to every grade together.
We laugh and joke in our own Colleen language. We have a very special bond because we share the same name. Just the other day her Mom yelled, "Colleen!" and we both yelled, "What?" back simultaneously. Then we crack up and look at each other and say, "Ok, who is going?" This has been going on for more than five decades now. The message is: Know yourself.

(Colleen's Big Brother likens himself to the thoughts of Mr. Oscar Wilde) Know what makes you happy and know what you do not need. Know what is important to you.

Everyone does not need to have children or have 5 if you wish. Everyone does not need to marry or marry every decade if you wish. Everyone does not need to have a pet or have 7 if you wish.

It is ok. Do what is best for you. Do what you can afford! Have the life you need, for you. A life that You are proud to call your own.

"One should always be in love,
that is the reason
one should never marry."
(9)
Now friends, come on now!
Everyone must have one incorrigibly irreverent friend.

Well, big brother was on to something. Marriage might not be right for everyone but love certainly is.

Big brother is one who knows exactly what he wants. He knows he loves his country, his two daughters and now his grandchildren, every day, like there is no tomorrow.

My other friend wrote to me a vision of an imagined love affair with a truly imagined soulmate. If you love yourself, you will attract exactly the right kind of person. And all will become possible for you.

> "There she stood,
> Waiting, Wanting, Wishing He would look her way.
> What he didn't know is...
> she had rehearsed this moment a million times before Now it was here.
> Will it happen the way she dreamed? He saw her, and he smiled.
> As he walked her way, she nearly froze. It was him... He was the one.
> Finally, he will love her, too.
> There he stood, right in front of her, just a breath away...
> His eyes were somehow
> not as bright as she'd imagined,
> he wasn't as charming as she had seen him all those times in her dreams.
> His words were not as eloquently spoken... Alas, this was
> not the man of her dreams, not her destiny at all.
> She was in love with love...
> not the man but the dream of love.
> So precious, so pure."
>
> —A vision of love by Jodi Lee Curtis

Casillo
Easy lesson here: Love of self – Imagination is all you need!

Chapter Six

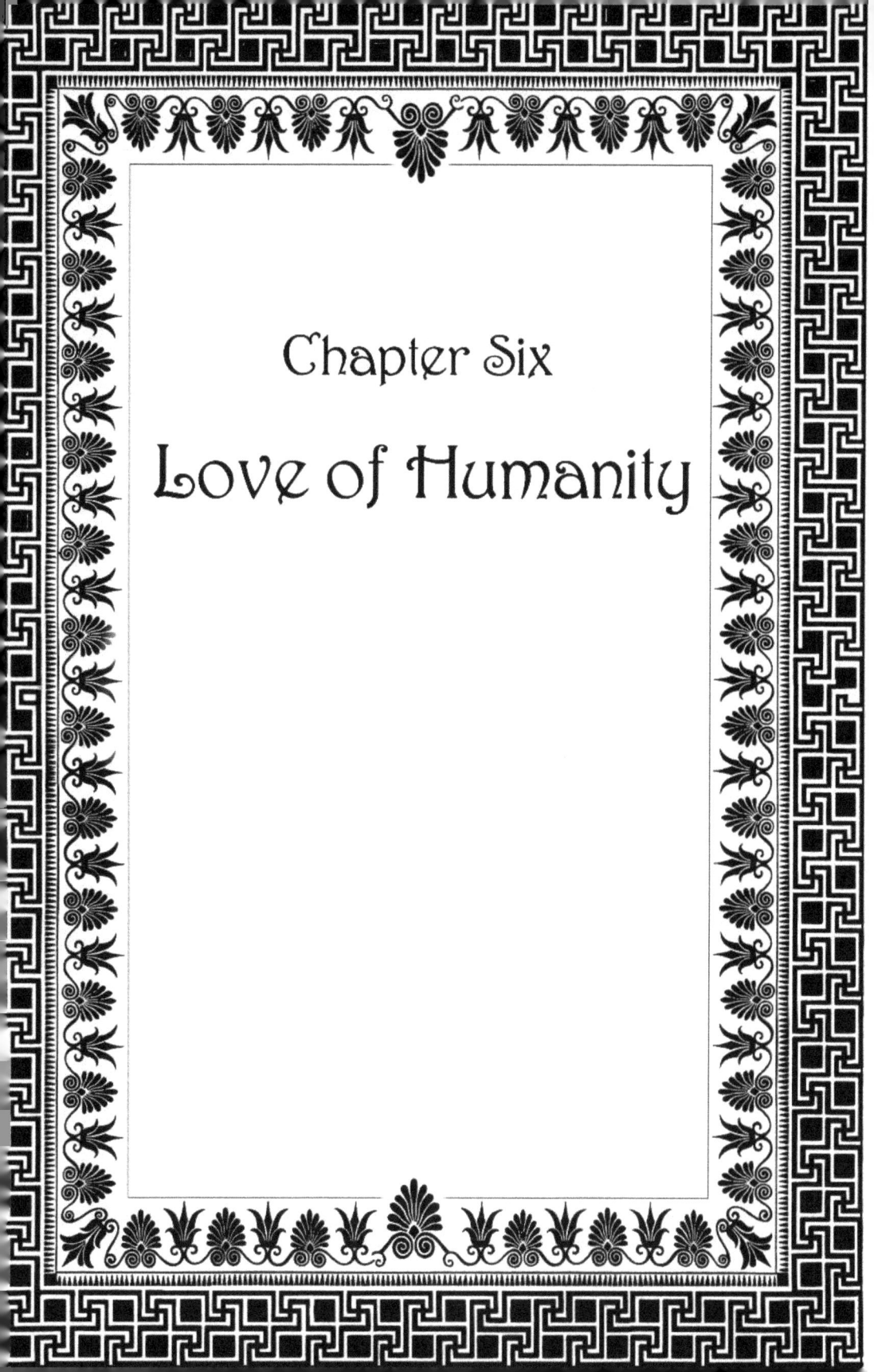

Love of Humanity

Far Away Beach

Far-Away Beach

Is there anything better than being a little kid and going on
vacation to the seashore?
I remember thinking all of humanity was there to bask
in the rays of sunshine and breathe in the sea air.
Everyone is joyously in love with their precious time away.
We would swim for hours each day and
then ride our bicycles until sunset.
As a child, I was always impetuously waiting,
and *Far Away Beach* conveys
the seemingly arduous journey
from the car to the ocean.
It seemed to take forever.
Finally, once you were there, everyone was
celebrating and full of laughter.
Everyone plays at the beach.
Young or old, everyone plays and has fun.
People are kind to each other and
share with each other all day long!
I love humanity and approach every human
as another chance to make a friend.

*"One Love, one heart, let's get together
and feel alright."*

One of the founders of the 1960s and 1970s musical revolution known as the genre called Reggae is Singer/Songwriter, Mr. Bob Marley.

Mr. Marley spoke to a generation. He changed our way of viewing the world. The spirit of Reggae is about feeling the words and speaking truths using song. He lived in a tumultuous time in Jamaica. The times were ripe for change. He did not believe violence was ever an answer. He made you believe a "revolution within your mind" was possible.
Simply, one love, one heart was possible and could become a way of life. One Love should be a cause for celebration every day.

> *"People can you feel it? Love is everywhere. " "People can you feel it? Love is everywhere. " "People can you feel it? Love is everywhere. "*

(The above passage is from a song called, "Revival" by the Allman Brothers Band)

We are travelers on a cosmic journey,
stardust, swirling and dancing in the eddies and whirlpools of infinity. Life is eternal.
We have stopped for a moment to encounter each other, to meet, to love, to share.
This is a precious moment.
It is a little parenthesis in eternity.

-Paulo Coelho, The Alchemist

Paulo Coelho is one of my favorite authors. Enjoy all his works as you carry on through this journey to unconditional love.

He employs many different methods to teach a person about love and caring for our Mother Earth.
Love of humanity teaches us:

> *"If you want to awaken all of humanity, then awaken all of yourself.*
>
> *If you want to eliminate the suffering in the world, then eliminate all the negative and dark within yourself.*
>
> *Truly, the greatest gift you have to give is that of your own self-transformation."*

- From Hua Hu Ching, and in gratitude (10)

Try, try, try again.

Here is a quote to further the point of awakening yourself in order to help awaken humanity:

"Love is the answer to everything.

It's the only reason to do anything. If you don't write stories you love, you'll never make it.
If you don't write stories that other people love, you'll never make it."

This was written by award winning science fiction author, Ray Bradbury in a motivational piece about the art of writing.

Another of Ray Bradbury's quotes speaks about loving humanity, loving yourself and being in love with loving. Absent of any fear.

"If we listened to our intellect, we'd never have a love affair. we'd never have a friendship.
We'd never go into business, because we'd be cynical. Well, that's nonsense.

You've got to jump off cliffs all the time and build your wings on the way down. "

Love of humanity – Seeing all as one universal loving group of humans

"If I could give you one thing in life, I would give you the ability to see yourself through my eyes. Only then would you realize how special you are to the world."

If only I could give every child this feeling to hold in their hearts.

Unjustly, too many children grow up without ever feeling the warmth of unconditional love that flows through each of us.

Sensitive, deep and compassionate people are needed here on Mother Earth, yet "beautiful people" do not just happen.

Beautiful people have usually known defeat. They have known suffering, struggle, and they have known exploitation and loss.

Beautiful people persevered and found their way out of the depths. Beautiful people appreciate life. They live it in the moment.

Beautiful people understand life and balanced concern for others. A beautiful person knows the worth of living in compassion, gentleness. You can easily see their countenance is full of deep love.

Love of humanity shows us the simple things in life:

> *Every time you smile at someone, It is an action of love,*
> *A gift to that person, A beautiful thing.*
>
> - Message from Mother Teresa,
> a Catholic Nun from Calcutta India (6)

Kindness is something taught as a virtue in every religion, every country, and every city. Kind acts are easy to spread and should be made readily available for the asking. Wouldn't it be a much better world?

There is a reason for each person who comes into your life.
Either you need their love or they need yours.
Either you will change their life or they will change yours...
or maybe both lives will change.

To further this thought, consciously balance the interaction between you:

Give what is needed and take what is required.

This will lead to kindness, eventual trust and ultimately to love.

If you love someone,
showing them is better than telling them. If you stop loving someone,
telling them is better than showing them.
People, please pay attention. If you stop loving someone, tell them. Face it and heal (yes, I said "heal" not "deal") with them.
Do not leave open wounds. It is not fair to everyone around you.

Unfortunately, even though you might want to imagine yourself there sometimes, you do not live on an island alone.

For advice, I would say the following: Be patient and keep your dignity and grace in every thought.

Dig for the innate grace resulting from loving and trusting the universe, and thoughts will soon turn to the future
and to new things and new people.
Each encounter leads you to another destiny- I promise it will. Just breathe deeply and just speak the truth.

Use your speech to express your heart and there will be peace.

His Holiness the 14th Dalai Lama of Tibetan Buddhist tradition tells us of compassion and kindness in all actions.

He says:
"The planet does not need more successful people.
The planet desperately needs more peacemakers,
healers, restorers, storytellers,
and lovers of all kinds."

Dalai Lama wrote a whole book about Compassion because compassion leads to kindness which leads to Love. We all need more love in our lives, I firmly believe this to be of clear evidence in this world.

With the deepest gratitude to the 14th Dalai Lama. Thank you. When the book was edited, my editor did not want me to say Namaste to you because she believes it to be a Hindu word.

So, I smiled. And then chuckled at how grateful I am for being on this earth with you. I am certain The 14th Dalai Lama is not concerned with how I go about loving humanity completely; he would be only concerned to know that I am trying to love every chance I get.

Fortuitously I witnessed the 14th Dalai Lama in person in Central Park in New York City. I listened to his speech in Central Park and then I saw him again coming down the street to his hotel. It was an indescribably magical moment in time.

To me, Namaste means;
"God who has filled my soul recognizes God who has filled your soul."

I do not believe his Holiness would have a problem with that sentiment in any language.

This is an everyday example of one of the very complex religious belief systems anchored in the devoted following of The Buddha. The Buddha was said to be a mortal who attained enlightenment during his lifetime on earth. He achieved the ability to cast off his mortal bonds to become immortal. He differs from Jesus Christ, who is a true Son of God and therefore a God visiting earth.

Buddhism has grown into many sects and is practiced in many different countries.

The 14th Dalai Lama is the leader of the Tibetan Buddhist population in exile in India today.

Another form of Buddhism is the Mahayana Buddhism created in Japan. This form of Buddhism aims at enlightenment by direct intuition through meditation.

Using basic words, Zen Buddhist practices can be described as a total state of focus that incorporates a complete state of togetherness between body and mind.

In modern day, mainstream media, Zen has become synonymous with a "a peaceful and balanced way of being".
Zen has also become a "state of mind" you can adopt.

To live in a Zen moment of life is to drop all illusion and see things without distortion caused by interference from your conscious mind. (11)

A Zen To-Do List

1. Do one thing at a time
2. Do it slowly and deliberately
3. Do it completely
4. Do less
5. Put space between things
6. Develop rituals
7. Designate time for certain things
8. Devote time to sitting
9. Smile every day and serve others
10. Make cleaning and cooking become meditation
11. Think about what is necessary
12. Live simply

Chapter Seven

In Love with Loving

CHAPTER SEVEN – IN LOVE WITH LOVING

"Lady Lounging" at Big Sur

My time spent touring the California coast was full of crazy, mind expansive, all-encompassing love. My heart was so full of loving thoughts that suddenly, everything became possible, just by imagining it.
Lady Lounging came about when I painted a landscape and decided to try a new silver paint in the palate. It brought me into a space where fantasy and reality mixed into one gorgeous land formation.

Then, serendipitously, a shape formed and became a woman on the beach (or "of" the beach), resting and enjoying the warm rays of the sun and the breeze off the water. There is magical love found overlooking the Pacific Ocean.

In this painting, being in love seemed to create more love as my mind remembered the precious warmth of love.

Out of all ten chapters, these words were easy to come by. The thoughts of loving flowed readily from me.
Then the thoughts became easy to make sit and stay.

My problem was time. I was writing in every stolen moment. With eager anticipation of all the loving thoughts to be conjured, while my rescue cat (now spoiled rotten and on the mend) tried desperately to get into the room by opening the door on his own. He was foiled for a good, long time and had quite a game of the attempt.

As I am now singing to him as I type "Ok my kitty cat, my baby boy, my good baby boy…. just one more page for Momma…please oh please baby boy."

Please enjoy my thoughts, as you can probably tell, I am incorrigibly in love with loving.

To start out right we shall say a little prayer for love. Prayer can be many different things.
To me, it is simply our conscious intent to connect to the universe, to share in the divine, immortal energy of love. The Holy Spirit lives in me and my devotion is to the cherished divine savior Jesus Christ.

Unconditional love is God's love.

There can be many spiritual and religious paths. At any one time in history there have been clergy, yogi, bodhisattvas and awakened spiritual leaders who graced this world with unconditional love.
Today there are approximately 5500 different religions, can you imagine? They all believe the same thing.
Belief in God and belief in one love.

We will use Vedic tradition to start off our journey. Let us rejoice:

Blessings in this world; reverence to your mother. A Blessing; reverence to your father.
A Blessing in the world; reverence to a contemplative.
A Blessing; reverence for a Brahmin. A Blessing into old age is a virtue.
A Blessing; conviction established. A Blessing; discernment attained.
The non-doing of evil things is a blessing. Dhammapada, 23.

To manifest love,
pray for love, live love, give love and accept love.

Be one with love
and my belief is you will attract similar souls.

To me,
making someone safe,
placing someone above your own needs, is an act of more love,
not less.

As my friend Nina so aptly put it,
this is the one exception to the "less is more" rule!

"Love is a sweet breeze that tickles your feelings when you think you have shut your heart tight."

"Love is an unexpected guest that doesn't even knock on the door and just invades your soul without asking permission."

I would say these are two different ends of the spectrum of love.

One is humanity loving each other and the other is romantic love-
wild and unsettling as it may seem at times.

Every time I approach you, it is a brand-new moment. Unconditional love is always my goal.
My every interaction is sacred, a moment to create a memory,

a fondness a bond
and finally trust

There is always a wonderful beginning to love,
whether we find others who reflect our feelings and ideas now, or we find a piece of ourselves in them.

Then there are fearless romantics, who look for authentic genuine love. They pursue it, although at times it can be outlandish, all- consuming and very inconvenient.
(I do call this the "honeymoon" stage, every relationship potentially can grow into full bloom if nurtured correctly)

Fatefully, It is true, there is a, "Can't Live Without Each Other" love You can achieve it through honesty and perseverance.

My wish for each of you is to obtain this goal and then perpetually sustain this achievement!

"Turns out, the millionth kiss Is even better than the first"

I thought this sentiment from a Valentine's Day card
was too sweet
not to be in a book about love.

My wish for all of you
is to find your "millionth kiss".

**Be weird. Take chances. Try new things. Be Who You Are.
Because you never know,**

Who would love the person you hide.

Love is giving someone the power to destroy you... but trusting them not to.

This is a very hard concept to follow. Why give up security of spirit? Do not give up spirit. Give up desire. Give up longing.
In a satiated state one can then give up.

You need to have a best friend and a soul mate, so, you know what true love feels like.
It is the kind without strings - without expectations, or the need to measure up.
It is not seeing each other every day and loving anyway.

It is felt when you look into their eyes and be aware of nothing else.
It isn't judging - it feels like you've found the person who makes life on Mother Earth, fun.
They complement you in every way you fall short - or they share the shortcoming with you.

This came from my longtime friend and great business colleague. Love you Kate! Thank you, for being part of this crazy ride and thank you for your part of my journey.

Don't love too soon
Don't trust too fast
Don't quit too early
Don't expect too much

These thoughts came from an Emergency Room nurse.
She has a unique perspective as a serious practitioner regarding real time human frailties of everyday life and death.
She also sees the consequences of
bad choices, bad decisions and Karma firsthand.

Don't love too soon
(I would add - Every seed planted, will grow, then blossom in its own season.)

Don't trust too fast
Trust in yourself and your instincts and listen to them. Your instincts will guide you to the right situations.

(My friend Dean said it the other day. If you are struggling to make the other person love you as you need to be loved, it is not the right relationship. If you are struggling to make the relationship work to enhance the love and commitment
and you are willing to do anything to complete yourself with the person, I believe then you are in the right relationship.)

Don't quit too early
Quitting is not an option; it is a choice. People meet and interact with others for many reasons,
some for long periods of time, or short periods of time.

Trust intuition match it against your motivation, then decide what is best. Not what is best for you in this moment, but what is best for both persons involved overall.
What would promote the most peace and unconditional love?

Some people are meant to be close to you at a point in time. They don't leave, they just enter into a different place in your heart.
I like to think of it as my "Immortal Archives of Love".

Don't expect too much
I agree.
My belief is one of mortality. One of my best girlfriends, (friends since I was 14 years old at the roller-skating rink), so aptly put it,
"you will only live as long as you are supposed to live"

Part of living life is to enjoy every moment, treasure every person, animal and plant you meet.

I would not trade my new and upcoming experiences for anything in the world.

If you truly love someone, then the only thing
you want for them is to be happy.
even if it is not with you.

Please enjoy the pleasure of
selfless love and unconditional love.

If I can bring it to your attention, and I can help you to manifest it, then I have succeeded in my reaching my goal of immortality.

Use your own feelings to understand the role the person played in your life. You will understand then where they need to be.
Even if it is away from you. Wish them well and you will be well, too.

I am very busy loving the people
who love me so I truly do not have time to worry about
who may not like me.

Love should flow freely.
Free will should make it flow as it should. Free will should take precedence overall,
as it is our unique characteristic, here on Mother Earth.

If the flow of energy/love is constricted, then the path eventually and ultimately will change, as it cannot sustain itself when constricted.
If it is constricted too long, the path will change to accommodate the flow, but it will not be ideal,
there will be consequences to the trees and fish.
It is simple, yet people spend their lives trying to change the flow. The flow goes where it is meant to, it is up to you to adjust your path or find a new stream.

Chapter Eight

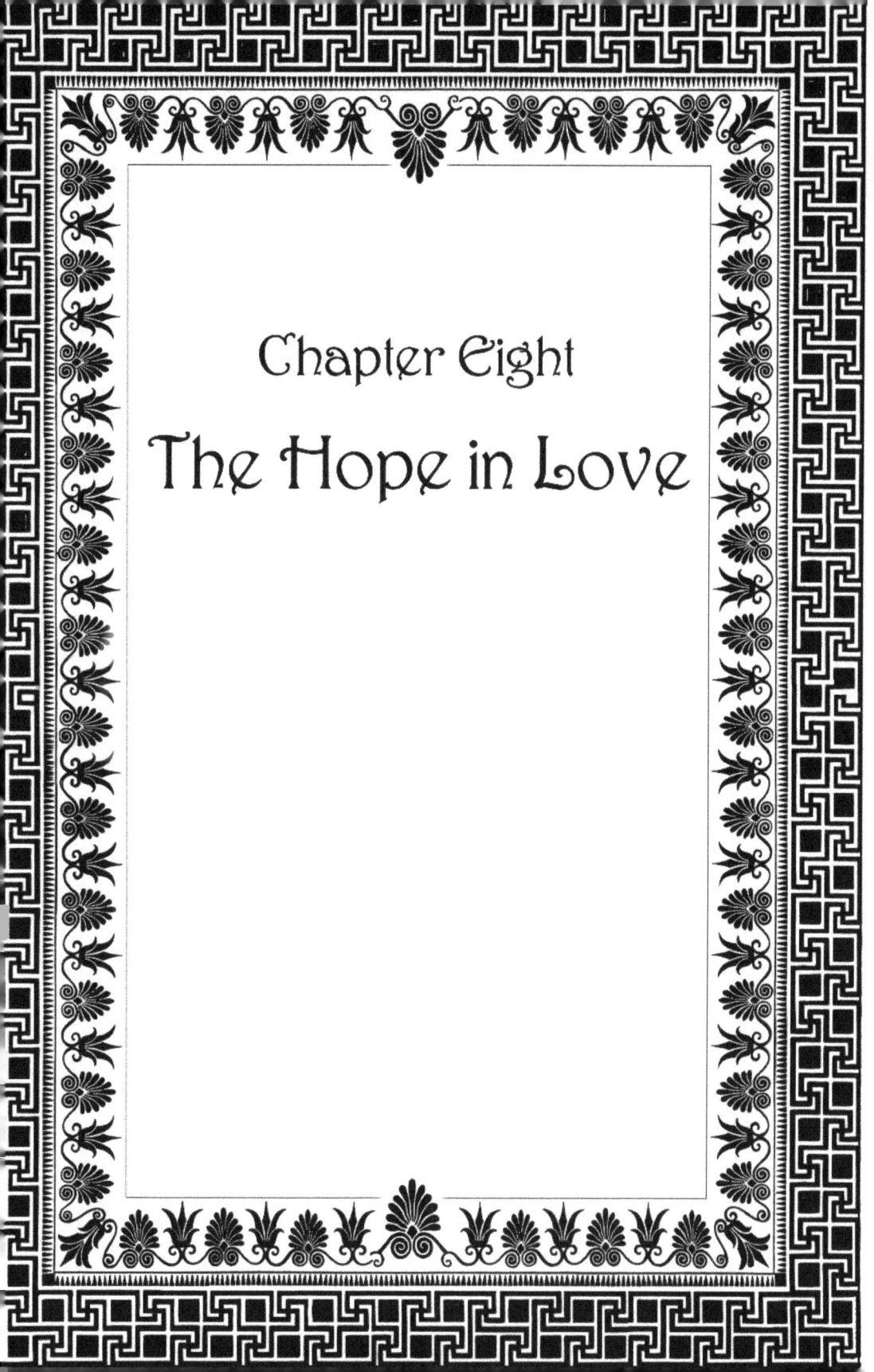

The Hope in Love

Jeremy's Tree

Jeremy's Tree and Jeremy's Forest
represent the hope of life, the hope of nature's eternal renewal.

The two paintings are, at the start, a tribute to a life cut tragically short by street drugs. It was a deep shock and a painful wound to those who dearly loved him. I would like to sincerely believe that love creates resilience.

Jeremy's Tree Original is 20"x16", acrylic on canvas

Jeremy's Tree shows no matter what lies ahead, the sun is always there to help guide you and to illuminate the possibilities. The colors are peaceful, and the forest is tranquil. Jeremy's Tree is a good tree; it is strong and supple and embedded solidly in the earth. Please remember Jeremy as this tree. Just as Jeremy was embedded solidly in the love of his parents, friends, and family.

I sent out a request to my family and friends to share the feelings evoked when viewing Jeremy's Tree, this was their response:

"Reminds me of Christmas joy, the smell of pine trees
and pinecones, balsam, and fires burning. It makes me think that art is such a wonderful gift and brings joy and happiness to the artist and the viewer."

Jeremy's Forest

Jeremy's Forest became a painting because I had paint left on the palette. The colors in Jeremy's Trees were so beautiful. I wanted to continue creating a sky full of color and wonder. A sky full of future and love and comfort.

I created a path to walk, and a goal to attain. The goal is deep in the tranquil forest, where only love remains. It reminds me of the journey on the path to happiness.

When it was finished, I sent out a request to my family and friends to share the feelings it evoked when viewing Jeremy's Forest.

My cousin sent an "Evocation from family: " Having spent an on-and- off night camping atop a cliff, when peeking over the edge, it seems the morning light cutting through the tail of the disintegrating cloud system, tells me, after a cup of fresh "cowboy coffee", it's going to be a perfect day. Climb on! "
Every new day brings a new chance.

"Hope is an orientation of the spirit, an orientation of the heart. It is not the conviction that something will turn out well, but the certainty that something makes sense, regardless of how it turns out."

Dedicated to a man who shaped my perception of the modern world, former President of Czechoslovakia, and author, and scholar, Vaclav Havel

If you love someone and they love you, it is precious.
Treat it with care, grow
then use that reality, that mindset; (the understanding two people have as they treat each other with love), to forge out in the world together.

Allow hope to form- hope for a better day.
A better way can be developed because of their hope of unconditional love within each other, and each person's conviction to love.

There is no such thing as defeat, as long as you keep trying.
Trust is built through consistency over time.

Some thoughts here were sent by my friend who used to ride the school bus with me to elementary school. We reconnected recently and found nothing had changed. We were still riding the school bus, only the classes were harder, and the ride was longer.
I love her spirit and determination; it inspires me to try, too.

My choice is to believe my version of a teaching from a Chinese philosopher,

"If you fall down 7 times,
make sure you stand back up 8 times"

There is always another chance to change things as long as you are still alive.

*"Love comes to those who still hope, even though they've been
disappointed,
to those who still believe
even though they've been betrayed,
to those who still love
even though they've been hurt before."*

-Author Unknown

Same truth demonstrated in very different quotes.

"Giving of one's own heart without an ulterior motive is the act of real love."

To me, they both express the same concept. This concept takes root in a metaphysical truth - as it is above, so it is below.

My point is simple. Intent creates reaction. Hope is part of loving. Unconditional love springs naturally from hope. There is unconditional love in hope.
Just Be. Be true to who you are. Be true to your good nature. Love and altruistic intent for all Mother Earth's creatures can be nurtured where kindness is present. Kindness leads to love.

*"If you have given up hope of ever being happy, cheer up.
Never lose hope.
Your soul, being a reflection of the ever-joyous Spirit, is, in essence, happiness itself"*

-Paramahansa Yogananda on Happiness

When you love with your whole heart, you must run the risk of giving without getting back the same.
Let's face it. Relationships sometimes end.
Sometimes, when a relationship starts passionately, it leaves you the worse for wear. You feel so tired, your heart heaves and feels physically damaged. You feel your ability to love has diminished. Yet, you go on breathing, just existing. But I have a different belief.

My belief is your heart is detached from the reason they left. Your heart knew they needed to leave you alone. They were keeping you from enjoying the adoration and happy moments you deserve. You knew they could not fly with you anymore.

The pain you feel is your emotional self, questioning why it ended, and whether it was your fault.

It really does not matter why it ended. Someone needed to learn something.

Some relationships are meant to end, they were meant to serve a specific purpose. In relationships, sometimes one partner will not change and will stop growing. That person will not change in life, nor for the sake of love.
You cannot expect someone to share, when they cannot. It is just not possible.

So, you see, if you expect change, expect to help in the transformation. In other words, you must change too. When you cannot change enough for your partner without risking the loss of yourself, then you must move on.

It is a simple formula really.

My Dad has a saying,

"Whatever effort you do in life; it better do one of two things:

1. It better make you money or
2. it better make you happy.
3. If something does not do one of those things, don't do it! "

**If the sun's too sad to shine,
and Fate restores our souls untwined, Just remember:
Once, for a heartbeat, your heart held mine, Your hand, So many oceans
From its heart-stopping farewell caress, in mine, One more time,
one last time...
no more time...no last kiss, one last wish:
My wish for me,
mirrors my wish for thee, My precious love,
with loves' final breath, in love? ... are we?**

- Dave B.

My friend from high school wrote this passage.
He is such a romantic, isn't he?
Hope in love is sometimes accepting a loss and moving on into peace.
All of life needs a balance. Peace leads to balance and a possible future.

My friend loves to write, and he weaves all sorts of emotions into stories of the heart. He is incredibly careful who he weaves into his life's tapestry.

After reading this, I asked him about why he wrote these words. What does it really mean to you? Here is his answer.
"In this case, it's a statement of surrender, sometimes "fate" will take what it will and perhaps it allows the peace coming from acceptance of it"

*   *   *

Do not hesitate. Love, and then worry about the rest later. It is worth it.

What if you were weaving your life fabric and decided to pick a nice bold thread, But, after a while, the thread was too big and interfered with the nice pattern you had going, so you plucked it out.
You do not have to hate or burn or dread that thread! It is a nice enough thread. It just does not fit in with you. Do not abandon all your threads.

Rather, save it for later when you might want a border? Life changes, people have things they need to do.
Unconditional Love flows from hoping for a better world. Only Hope can lead to better days.

Love is from the divine. God is Love.
The divine immortals consist of unconditionally loving energy flowing abundantly throughout
every bit of matter and cell in the universe.

Love flows freely, and infinitely. Love is, and will always,
remain endless and ever present.

Loving kindness will make you immortal. You will not be forgotten.

The hope in love is the love of the divine. The hope and belief in the universal truths of love and kindness.
The hope it will lead you on the right path. A path to nurture your soul.

* * *

Now, back to relationships; when one partner chooses
to reject your love, not using your love for their own betterment, then
what have you really lost?

Serve your highest purpose by surrounding yourself with unconditional love.
Some will fall away, but those who stay
will be steadfast and true people.

How can we not hope?
We know love is everywhere, Ever-present,
and open to all sentient beings.

Yes, to every living creature. So how can we not hope?
We are alive!

The nice thing about every single day is that
no one has ever used it before; it is brand new.

This idea is printed on a calligraphy wall hanging in my Mom's house. Isn't it a wonderful thought? Each day is another new opportunity. Each day begins and it ends. Then, a new day is born, and another chance is unveiled.

No one has used the day; therefore no one can spoil it. Unless you decide to allow them to spoil it. Or if fate chooses to spoil it to teach a lesson.

Always give yourself new horizons, new goals. Always look for a new chance.
Always, Just Be...

Love lifts you beyond what you can bear.

My friend and I discussed what this passage meant. We decided you are not alone when you have loved ones in your life. They give you hope. If you think of the well wishes and dreams your loved ones have for you, the future will come alive with their intent. If you only believe...

My truth is, we only have love. It is logical to have hope, since hope leads to love. Just Be, There is Only One Love.

Chapter Nine
Devoted to the Immortal

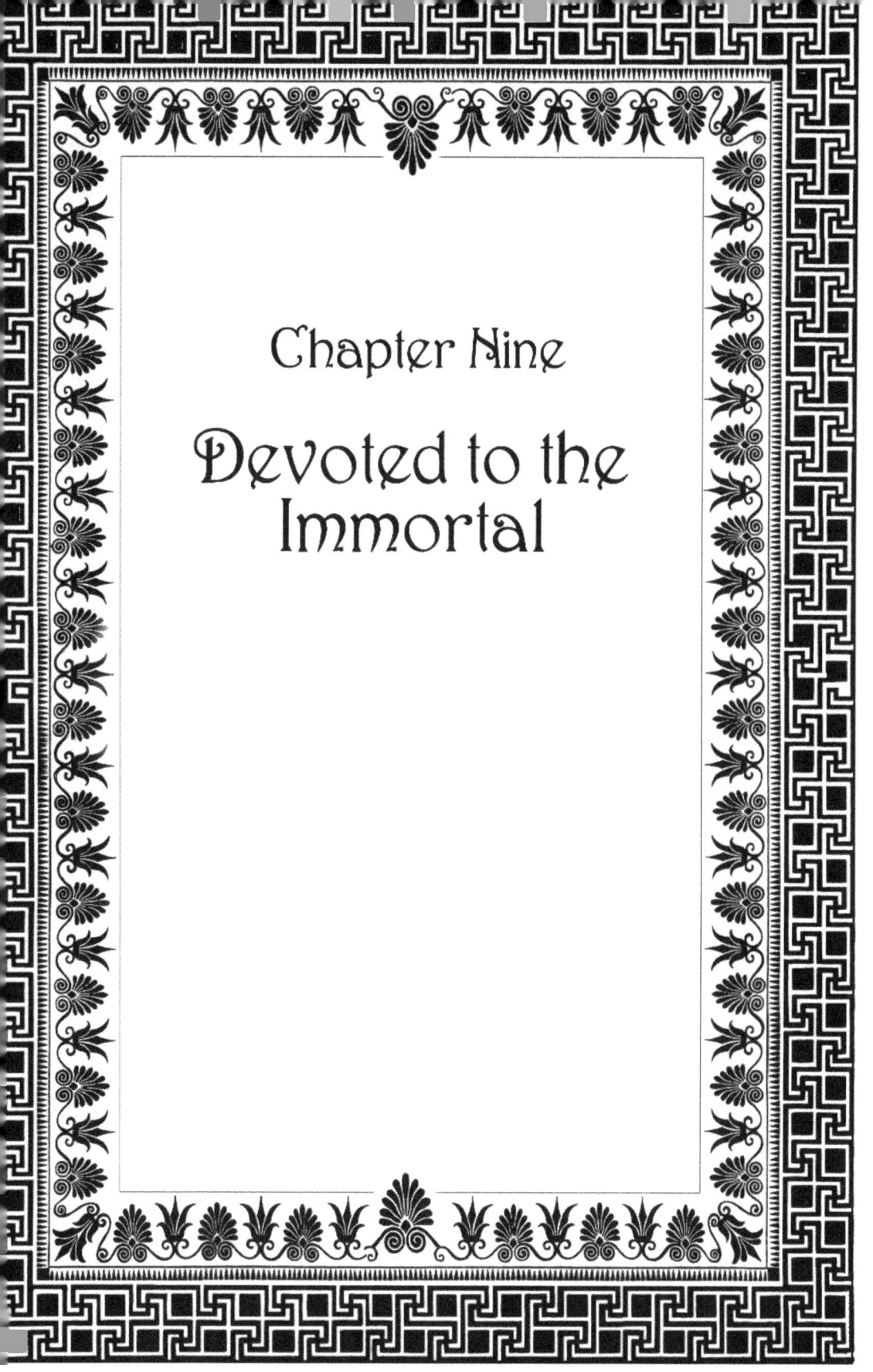

INFINITE IMMORTAL

INFINITE IMMORTAL (Australian Rain Forest)
Original is 24" x 18", acrylic on canvas

To me,
This view of an Australian Rain Forest exemplifies Immortal love.
The example set here is;

deep and serene
and meaningful and empty
and full of contentment as immortality itself.
It is ever-rejuvenating,
creating immortality in its very existence.

**O Lord, our Lord,
how excellent is Your name in all the earth!**

— Psalm 8:9

This passage was suggested to me by my childhood friend who happens to follow Judaism. She and I love the Lord with every breath, yet we use different languages and different methods to show our devotion.

One truth is clear, we do not care how you get to the place of eternal comfort and unconditional love. We just hope you try until you do.

There is only one God. God is unconditional love.

Grant me the strength to focus, to be mindful and present,
to serve with excellence, to be a force of love.

"To love...
for the sake of being loved... is human, but To love...
for the sake of loving...is angelic"

— Attributed to Alphonse Marie Louis de Prat de Lamartine (4)

My friends, these words by Lamartine are true.
We all owe much gratitude to The Immortals. (Immortals=God)

There is only one universe. In our universe there are humans and other living creatures. How can we not be all connected?

This is my dedication to The Immortal-my dear sweet God and all the envoys. Regardless of the form of religion giving you a path. Find a religion or knowledge level to get you to our one God, just get there. Just Be.

I wish us all to extend deep and abiding gratitude to all the deities and angelic beings, thank them for their constant presence enlightening and enlivening our souls.

" Love... surrounds every being and extends slowly to embrace all that shall be"

This is written by Khalil Gibran. Gibran is one of the authors I admire. Some of his other works are The Prophet and The Madman. He was well received in his life. His works are important to the understanding of ancient vs. modern day philosophy. Human nature never does change.

The weave of my fabric was woven firmly into place with thoughts from Rumi and Khalil Gibran.

Through writing this story, I asked friends for their favorite passages. My friend wanted to share this passage with the world. Interestingly, she is deeply in love with the world. She regularly rescues animals.
Her heart had recently been wounded, but she choose to love the world unconditionally. She did not think of the pain in her heart, she just joined in and sent me her thoughts.
You see, she was grieving the loss of a brother who died too young. A sudden death is always more painful. We all know how it hurts to even think about deep love after such a profound loss.
Yet, she wanted me to have my dream!
She loves completely and continually, without question.

Friends, be assured kindness and love are the only true constants.

My friend owns and manages an animal rescue center.

She devotes every day to saving animals from dangerous situations and sometimes imminent death. She is living her dream and changing countless lives with her work. She will receive my fervent gratitude and as much help as I can give, forever, if she needs it.

*   *   *

The passage below is meant to be a lesson on how to tune into the true essence of your existence.
The true essence of your existence can never totally be obscured.

No matter how many "false faces" you show to the world, your true essence of your existence defines you and ultimately, what is in your heart will be revealed.

My wish is for us all to find divine love.
Divine love is where The Immortals live...

Enjoy. It is so pretty. It is a channeled message from Archangel Michael, a protector from the realm of Archangels.

> *"Your heart is the sacred portal allowing you*
> *to access the higher realms, allowing you in this moment,*
> *and in any moment,*
> *to tune into all that is,*
> *to tune in to divine love and light,*
> *to tune in to the still, peaceful gap, the void, the darkness,*
> *the stillness, the calm within"*
>
> *— Archangel Michael*

Your heart will lead you to all you desire simply by being open to the possibilities. This means the quieter you become, the more of yourself you will hear.

Stillness will give you peace, it will offer you a chance to see light through darkness. You will then allow yourself to grow to enjoy the feel of divine love found ever present, and unconditionally provided in and by the universe.

Namaste
(The light in me knows the light in you or The God in me sees the God in you)

Immortal love is pure love.

**"Pure love has neither boundaries nor barriers; it lifts you up when you are too weak to stand,
supports you when you are thrown off balance, encourages you when you are about to give up, and gives sustenance to help you thrive without ever asking for anything in return."**

These are thoughts from another friend. As children we played on the playground. Together, we can write another whole book! HA!

Two young girls playing on the school playground. As we have had our share of trials and tribulations through this life journey, it did not stop us. We still grew into highly intuitive and creative people who write things like this. This passage she wrote makes me grateful first, but also truly overwhelmed at how true it is.

Love asks for nothing in return. You can choose to love back or you can choose to receive it and just be grateful.

Either way, love perseveres. Love is immortal.

My wish for you is pure love. Pure unconditional love. Blessed Be!

Immortal love encompasses life and death. All that is born will someday die. Life is a cycle. There is no other reality.

I was a lucky kid. There were a lot of loving relatives in my family.
My Grandma's first cousin and her husband had no children, and I was the oldest of Grandma's grandchildren, therefore I became their surrogate grandchild.

My first job at 14, I cleaned their house as I asked Cousin Isabel no less than one million questions.
The stories she told me were very exciting. For her first job, she and all her cousins (including my grandma and her sister) worked on an assembly line rolling cigars in a cigar factory. She and her soon- to- be husband finally earned enough money to get married in 1931.
She and her husband were childhood sweethearts beginning at age 16. They were married for 65 years. They were very much in love.

My cousins lived in a two-story home. In the kitchen on the second floor we would watch the parakeets play and sing, as we picked cherries straight off the tree from the balcony.

We had lovely lunches. Cousin Frank would go out and buy everything fresh that day.

My Italian cousins used to switch languages on me. They would scheme what to get me for my "special lunch" without me knowing.

I grew to learn Italian just because I was nosy! And I wanted to know what they were bringing for the three of us to eat.

For me, it was a magical time.
The love they shared with me, made them immortal in my eyes.

Their love, guidance and friendship were a life lesson since they were both gone by the time I was 17.

Cousin Frank passed away very suddenly. I do not think Cousin Isabel ever came out of shock. Cousin Isabel was a faithful woman, she mourned but she never changed toward me. She was loving and kind and I felt completely special.
There was just something missing from us. It was Cousin Frank's happiness.

We missed the immortal joy of love from him.
After only a couple years, Cousin Isabel too, left me.

When she did, I wrote this passage for her. Please enjoy it.

If only I could learn before I die how to love as deeply as you. If a person has the great fortune to be loved by you, it is as though God has given that person a special privilege.
The unconditional breadth of your love wraps around the person and gives them a special strength.
This strength will allow the person to face pain and sorrow with head held high and shoulders squared. For each of us grew knowing no matter what, you, my family, loved us and will stand with us through it all.
You will watch over us through all our days.

My wish for my special cousin-
When the end of your road is near, my wish for you is to think of your life as a much resplendent beauty, from the love of your family to the sights of another sunset. May the awesome strength of your soul carry you gracefully into destiny. I thank you for being a part of my world and I beg you to always stay there.

My lesson at a very young age was one of life, love and the mortality of those we love. You learn heartbreak early when you discover
our grandparents and older relatives leave us, and our beloved pets do not live forever.

This is another reason to live in the moment. Enjoy every moment with those you love.

Attention: all living creatures-
I will love you
until infinity runs out.

You see, I determined long ago the truth, I cannot just love people.
I must love every living thing equally.

Only then do I become One.
Only then do I become one with the Immortals.
This, my friends is why I stress the importance of weaving your fabric of life with solid and strong fibers of love.
The fibers raise your being to a level of immortality.
Your fabric will exist long after your mortal body leaves us. My cousin Isabel and Frank's fabric still embraces me long after they are gone from my arms. As of today, I have spent three decades without them and still have the warmth of their love in my soul and the fabric of family woven into my life tapestry.

Another road to immortality is to love all creatures as you love yourself.

> *"Until one has loved an animal, a part of one's soul remains unawake."*
>
> — Attributed to Anatole France

(A French author who was 1921 Novel Prize Laureate)

Please always remember to appreciate the ecological balance of the animals, plants and waterways. If you do, it will be very difficult for you not to be in awe of this wonderful planet.

You will easily treat animals and our natural environment with as much respect as people.
In the home where I grew up, we had cats, dogs and an occasional rabbit. Animals have a shorter life cycle than people do, so we begin to learn life is special and precious.

As we go through life, each little creature allows us an understanding into their happiness and their struggles. This fosters knowledge of all life. Life is meant to be worshipped with love and kindness.

I have thought it particularly important in my life to
surround myself with "animal people".

To love an animal is to love something besides yourself, to give unconditionally, to nurture and support another life totally dependent on your own.

Truth be told, if a person is kind to animals, they probably have a good heart.
What I do not understand is when someone takes a life without having concern for that life. You should not take a life easily.

Live as though life is precious, and you will always make
the right decision for your soul.

If you find a person who is constant, awake to the inner light,
learned, long-suffering, endowed with devotion, a noble person
- follow this good and great person
even as the moon follows the path of the stars.

—the Dhammapada (3)- presents the details of these events and is a rich source of legend for the life and times of the Buddha

One path to immortality is to be devoted to enriching the lives of all around you. You will not need to go far from home to find those deserving of your unconditional love.

The quote from the Dhammapada reminds me of a precious friend. She is a cherished companion on this path. A gift of God. This lady's ordinary daily life is quite special as a public servant.
I have never met a more dedicated, constant, beautiful soul. If you are lucky to be in her presence, you are in her care.
She helps strangers every day,
she helps them just like she would help a loved one. She takes in animals, people, anything that needs love. For a reason, for a season, she is always there, constant, and true in her love.

To become an immortal is to live in unconditional love with God and all the universe.

To become immortal for someone else is to be explained as human love. The meaning of love that is called "true love".

> *"True love...*
> *has no beginning*
> *and no end..."*

True love is something different for every person. What does true love mean to you? Total acceptance? Devotion, like no other?

A love which created a bond where it did not make a difference whether we endured a good thing or bad thing.
We were devoted and loved like no other.

True love for extended family, true love of friends, true love for animals, true love for parents, true love for grandparents-
each is a different but special kind of true love.

Imagine an entire understanding of the sense of magic ever present in our majestic Mother Earth?
This is the joy of some people.

They will not lose their sense of magic. They believe in the triumph of spirit. They believe in the mystery of love.

They have experienced it
by looking into the eyes of their newborn children.
They have experienced it in the conflagrations of the heart (sometimes called "relationships).

This type of person's love is pure and true.

Our world would be greatly diminished without their continued optimism and ultimate innocence.

Chapter Ten

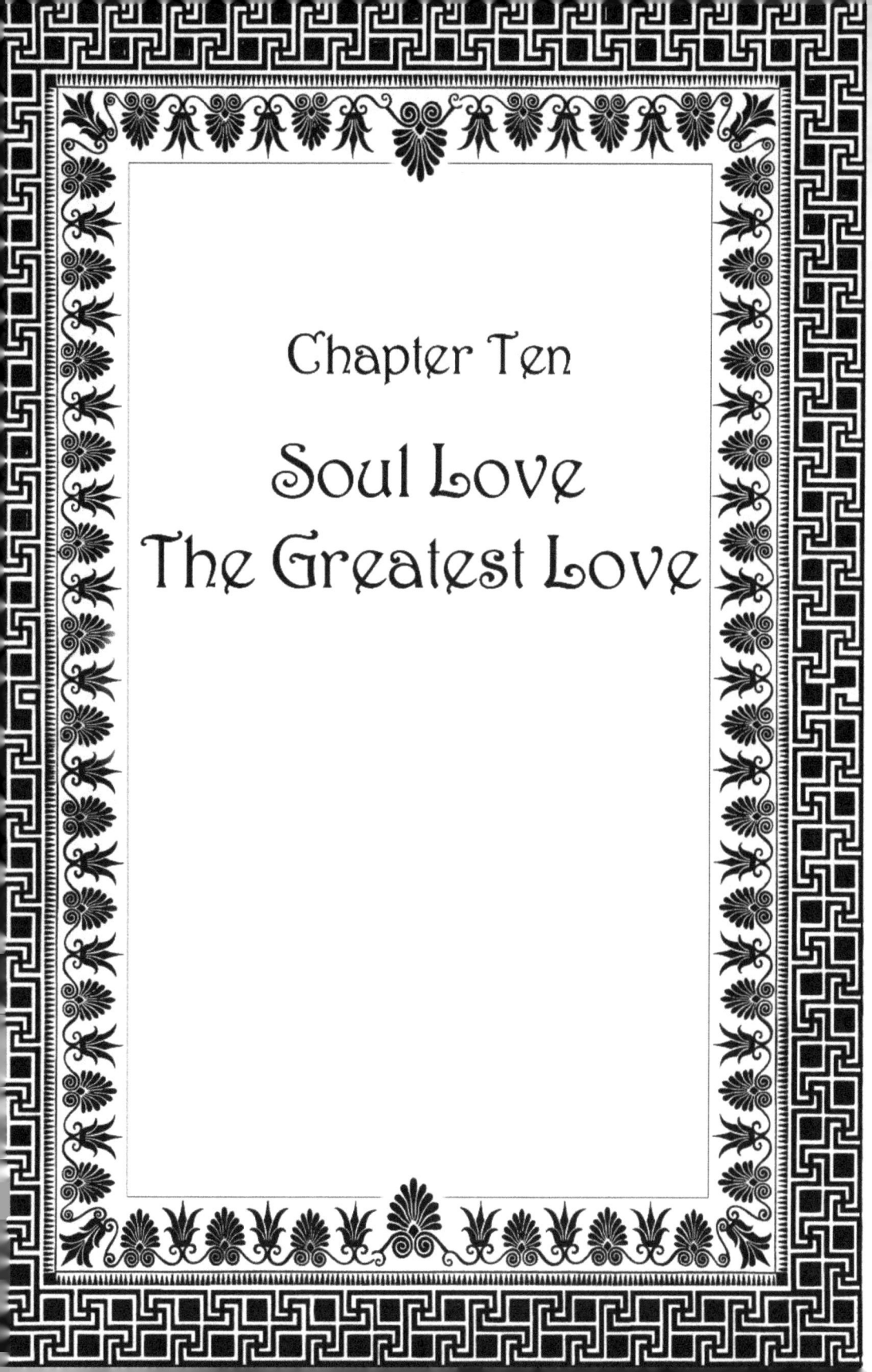

Soul Love
The Greatest Love

Frankie's Heart

Frankie's Heart

The soul of the Earth shows magnificent colors. If you look, you will see blue horizons of the future and a heart experiencing eternal love. It reminds me of what God created for us all: Love.

Frankie's mom saw my work and wrote:
"The painting is beautiful and heartfelt and was painted by my friend, who is loving and caring. The artist has suffered, herself, but loves others more than herself.
It reminds me of my daughter's blue eyes, the heart shape is the love I have for her and the love she had for me, the essence of God's love when he created all of us.
The white, billowing strokes in the painting remind me of clouds, heaven and a far distance. The huge heart coming over the mountains reminds me of how big my love is for my children and my grandchildren, Frankie and Leyla. It reminds me that love is endless and expansive. I feel having love and being loved is a true blessing."

The greatest love is infinite and all-encompassing.
Love can unite us into a feeling of familiarity with our fellow person. This love can lead directly to a feeling of family.
It provides a union with each soul you meet.

> *"If you have given up hope of ever being happy, cheer up. Never lose hope. Your soul, being a reflection of the ever-joyous Spirit, is, in essence, happiness itself"*
>
> — Paramahansa Yogananda on Happiness

> *"An invisible red thread connects those who are destined to meet, regardless of time, place, or circumstance.*
> *The thread may stretch or tangle, but it will never break."*
>
> — Chinese proverb

As you grow your family, your fabric becomes rich and your cloth becomes adorned with all the love of each individual.
Your fabric becomes supple and strong.
Hopefully, you begin to adorn your fabric-adding beautiful colorful threads along the way.
Sometimes, we lose a thread. Everyone is born to die. When that thread is pulled from our fabric,
it leaves a hole.
It is up to us to mend our fabric.
Just as others are tending to their own.

(I once knew a child whose family fabric was adorned with five generations of long-living relatives. We spoke about how blessed she was to know of her history and of her roots. Knowing her place in the family gave her a very rare sense of security and grace, even though she was a child of a divorce. The maternal connection is a deep bond.)

A tribute to greatest of love, soul love. Love of life itself. How cool is it when your friend leaves you these words on your voicemail or text message every time, he leaves a message?

"Loving you, Never Stop, Always"

This is a person who loves with his whole heart.
Yet, he spends time alone, not lonely, but solitary, as he does not allow the world's stressful people to disturb him.
If he spends time alone, it is because he will not have anything but real love in his life. He only will accept soul love, the unconditional love that grows over time and with patience.
As we discuss what a single life is, he admonishes me
and says "I don't do crazy" in his New York City accent. I giggle. He is noble, he is kind, and he is whole.
He is a person who can be your inspiration and a great strength. This type of person is God's gift of a real friend. He is a person I admire and has my unconditional love forever.

Life is for happy moments,
Off- the-beaten path adventures,
Summertime swims and all-night conversations.

My wish for you is to find another soul who will love to do simple things with you.
To have adventure just around the next turn, will always make life worth the struggle.

One of the greatest of all kinds of love is that of a child.

"Children believe their parents to be perfect, until you prove them wrong."

A cherished girlhood friend helped me write this. We were very little children, classmates in elementary school, all through Brownies and Girl Scouts. As I like to say, "we learned to be people together".
I love her very much. She is all that is good and loving and kind.
She has a sweetness that is contagious, and I value her immensely.

Once these words were spoken, boy, oh boy, they were immense. It is difficult to be a parent! As I told my Mom, the only reason I am not mad at you is there is no Rule Book! (just kidding)

This quote is dedicated to her daughter, Imani, whom she loves as she loves the universe. Imani is her soul and her world.

(A little side note here, "Imani" is translated as "Faith" in Swahili.)

Frankie's Heart
A greatest of love of all is love for a child.

You may notice, the painting "Frankie's Heart" is quite similar in concept to the "Maternal Nature" painting only in blue. When my friend Nina, Frankie's mother, saw the "Maternal Heart"
she asked if I could make it blue!?

Oy Vey! I said.
(truly afraid of abject failure during an attempt at re-creation).

Full onset panic mode now has me thinking quickly, so I create a thought like this, "But Nina, it is a painting, an artistic work, which will most likely never be duplicated again".
Instantly I knew, my explanation fell decidedly short. That it did not work, plain and simple. She began to explain in her way of explaining.

Only my friend since we were 14 years old, Nina can explain quite that way. You see, she is a "Jersey Girl" (an East Coast phenomenon where mixed cultures met at Ellis Island and created these incredibly beautiful combinations of children) with East Coast strut.

She is very theatrical, her mannerisms Italian, and her methods are *very* effective. One way or another, she manages to make me laugh. So funny I cry. Just hearing her voice starts me laughing sometimes.

This conversation was in person. Oh, I was cooked well done.

The truth of the matter was Frankie's favorite color was blue. Have you ever seen an Italian mother talk about her children? With these big eyes shining with the light of creation from above? It is a beautiful thing to behold.
So, of course, I painted a blue one and it didn't come out half bad! Nina's faith was strong enough for both of us.

Here is their story of Soul Love as it unfolded.

My dear friend sent her exuberant cheerleader, chronically asthmatic daughter to school, just like any other day. But her daughter, Francesca Marie had an asthma attack in last period gym class and died that day. The next day, her mother found this note Frankie had written to her.

Here for you to share too, is Frankie's note to her mom. The thoughts of an amazingly enlightened, kind and caring, 14-year-old girl. It is a mix of sayings from contemporary artists of her time.
Her thoughts were profound.

"As we grow up, we learn that even the
one person that wasn't supposed to ever let us down, probably will.
You'll have your heart broken
and you'll break other's hearts.
You'll fight with your best friend
or maybe even fall in love with them,
and you'll cry because time is flying by.
So take too many pictures, laugh too much,
forgive freely, and love like you've never been hurt.
Life comes with no guarantees, no time outs, no second chances.
You just have to live your life to the fullest.
Tell someone what they mean to you and tell someone off, speak out, dance in the pouring rain, told someone's hand, comfort a friend, fall asleep watching the sun come up. Stay up late, be a flirt and smile until your face hurts. Don't be afraid to take chances or fall in love and most of all; live in the moment because every second you spend angry or upset
is a second you can never get back".

— Frankie (Francesca Marie Previti)

How about we all make this our *New Year's Resolution* every year?

No more lives would be torn apart Wars would never start
Right would always win Time would heal all hearts
Everyone would have a friend Love would never end

In reading a blog by Rabbi Harold Kushner, I found a wonderful tribute to unconditional love of God. Please enjoy the never ending, all- encompassing feeling of one with our creator.

"God not only forgives our failures; He sees successes where no one else does, not even ourselves. Only God can give us credit for angry words we did not speak; temptations we resisted, patience, and gentleness little noticed and long forgotten by those around us. Such good deeds are never wasted and not forgotten, because God gives them a measure of eternity."

So, my friends, please know

Imagination is stronger than knowledge Myths are more potent than history Dreams are more powerful than facts Laughter is the cure for grief

Just Be, There is Only One Love.

Acknowledgements

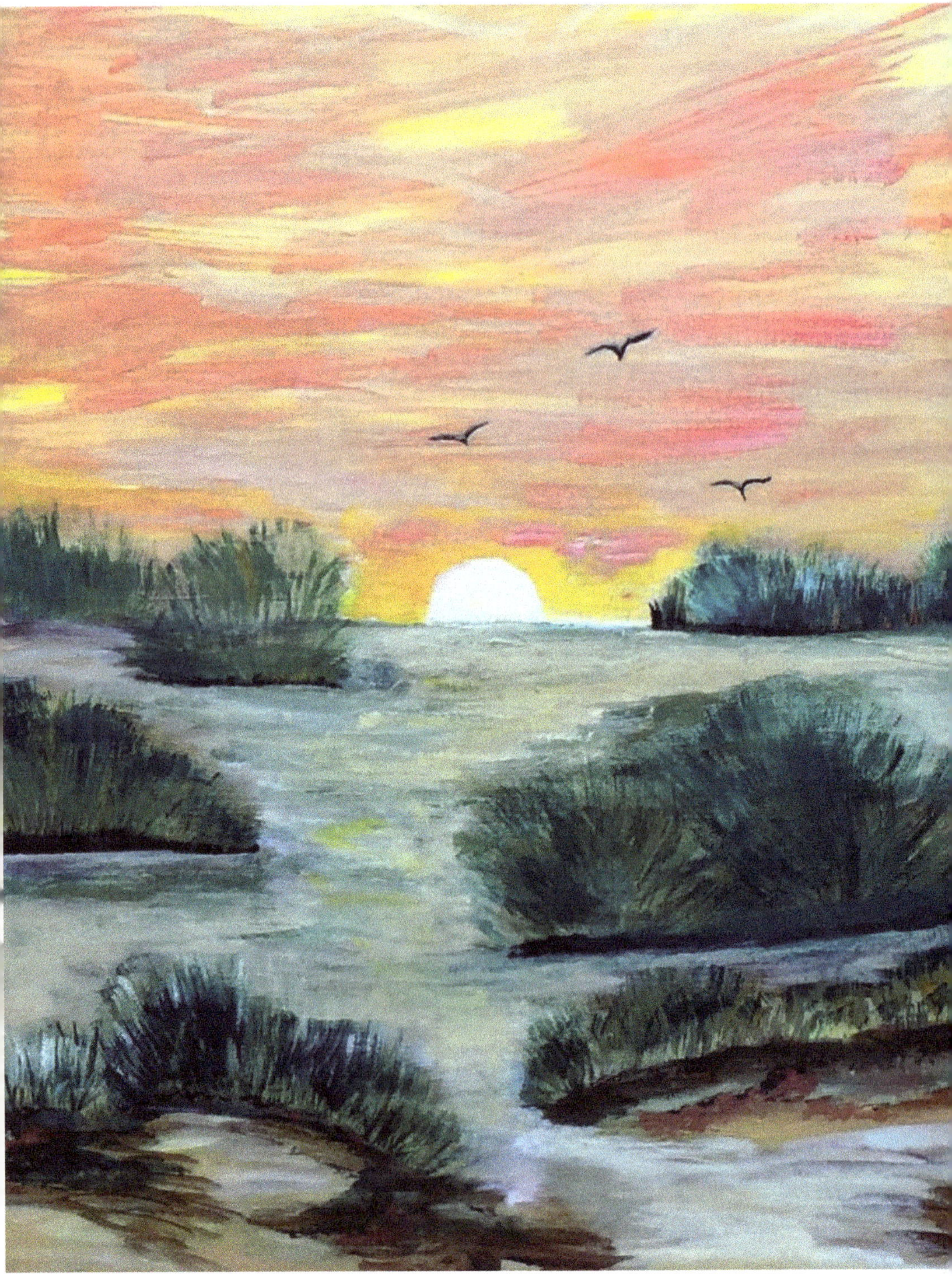

Joseph's Beach

Acknowledgements of good friends, happy memories

To me, Joseph's Beach shows us the sands of time may shape the landscape, but it is only temporary.
Each new landscape presents another chance to paint a beautiful memory.
Joseph is a boy who is kind and good. He was taken too soon, and I want to remember him well. He deserves it.
We will join together; and his family, friends and I will remember him. The beach is where his Mom lives now.

All that is born will eventually die, we must rely on individual destiny. I cannot seem to make sense of it all, so I choose to have faith in the divine plan.

Shout out to my MOMS! Kathleen Nugent. My Mom was a girl scout leader, an accomplished seamstress, a terrific cook and baker and she even found time to run a construction company with my family. She was a member of Zonta International, Moose Lodge and many other charitable organizations, taking leadership roles, as I watched.

She is stoic and brave and everything good. She never gives up, always stands by to help and she makes all of it look easy.

Thanks Mom & Dad and brother too…
I am blessed to have you with me this time around.

I wish to acknowledge James L. Hockenberry, Jim is the reason I even thought to write a book. He is a beloved friend and mentor and I value him dearly in my life.

Thank you to all my friends who I "tongue-in-cheek" call my "Lifers". Those friends are my "Tried and True Blues".
These are type of friends who drop the phone when you call because they are running out the door to come and help.

To all my childhood friends and to those, who were my classmates in school.
Each one of you contributed to this work.
Thank you, You all have enriched my life immeasurably.

END NOTES

Special thoughts and acknowledgements The Greatest Love- Dedications

This world lost Anne Coon during the time I was creating this book, so I decided to dedicate a couple moments to her memory. She was the quintessential social worker to the world.

Anne, the charity functions will never be the same without your enthusiastic participation. 400 Zonta wreaths, Crawford House Christmas decorations, you were the force of life.

Anne, I love you. Thank you for your life of service and thank you for your friendship.

My life would have been much less bright without you.

Kisses up to the sky Francesca, Alana, Joseph, Jeremy, Rendy, Chris, Caroline, Cousin Isabel and Cousin Frank All those mentioned here, always in our hearts.

This is my gift of assured immortality. You all mattered, really mattered. Camus the philosopher said this,

> **"Always go too far because that's where you will find the truth".**

Just Be, There Is Only One Love.

An inspirational book written ©Colleen Ann Nugent Artwork in book is original work ©Colleen Ann Nugent.

Descriptions in each chapter of the book are a visual representation of the sentiment expressed in each chapter. Some of the paintings are a dedication to loved ones, others are beautiful places.

Custom prints available in many sizes, custom sizes too.

Prints on high quality poster paper can be found at HN Book's sales portal: penswordpublishing.com

ABOUT THE AUTHOR

Colleen Ann Nugent spent many days in business, causing the business to earn money, but as an additional result, most of her work ended up being an aid in helping others.

It didn't start out to be that way, but it did end up that way.

This book was a natural progression from her paintings, which are featured in the book as the artwork.

During her career, she "did time" as a Child Support Enforcement Agent, a Personal Banker and an Operations Consultant.
None of this background had prepared her for the world of publishing, yet here, here is a book of love, happiness and peace.

I hope you enjoy reading this, as much as I did writing it.
Love & Light, Colleen

JUST BE,
THERE IS ONLY ONE LOVE
ENDNOTES

1. Rumi - The man, as per Wikipedia is :(Jalāl ad-Dīn Muhamma Rūmī, also known as Jalāl ad-Dīn Muhammad Balkhī, Mawlānā/Mevlânâ (مولانا), "our master"), and more popularly simply as Rumi (1207 – 17 December 1273), was a 13th-century Persian poet, jurist, Islamic scholar, theologian, and Sufi mystic) Sufism is a sect of Muslim.

2. Attributed to: Alphonse Marie Louis de Prat de Lamartine, chevalier de Pratz (October 1790 – 28 February 1869), a French writer, poet and politician.

3. the Dhammapada -scripture presents the details of these events and is a rich source of legend for the life and times of the Buddha The Dhammapad is a collection of sayings of the Buddha in verse form and one of the most widely read and best known Buddhist scriptures. The original version of the Dhammapada is in the Khuddaka Nikaya, a division of the Pali Canon of Theravada Buddhism.

4. "To Love...for the sake of being Loved... is human, but To Love... for the sake of loving...is Angelic" Attributed to: Alphonse Marie Louis de Prat de Lamartine

5. What you expect is defined by the mind, whereas the heart explores your unlimited potential. #haroldwbecker #thelovefoundation#unconditionallove

6. Mother Theresa is a Nun (a "Sister") from the Roman Catholic order who served the poor and homeless people of India, namely Calcutta. She is in line to be canonized by the Roman Catholic church.

7. You have to take care of yourself first. Before befriending others, you have to be your own friend. Before correcting others, you have to correct yourself. Before making others happy, you have to make yourself happy. It's not called selfishness, it's called personal development. Once you balance yourself, only then can you balance the world around you. Marcandangel.com (Angel and I discuss this in more detail in the "Self-Love" chapter of 1,000 Little Things, Happy, Successful People Do Differently.) "patience is the executioner of worry" ...Chapter 5 – Sanjay Kshetri: Author & Motivational Speaker

8. Written by Oscar Wilde. Oscar Fingal O'Flahertie Wills Wilde (16 October 1854 – 30 November 1900) was an Irish playwright, novelist, essayist, and poet. He is remembered for his epigrams, his novel The Picture of Dorian Gray, his plays, as well as the circumstances of his imprisonment and early death. Fluent in French and German early in life, he proved himself to be an outstanding classicist, first at Dublin, then at Oxford. He became known for his involvement in the rising philosophy of aestheticism, As a spokesman for aestheticism, he tried his hand at various literary activities: he published a book of poems, lectured in the United States and Canada on the new "English Renaissance in Art", and then returned to London where he worked prolifically as a journalist. Known for his biting wit, flamboyant dress and glittering conversation, Wilde became one of the best-known personalities of his

day. At the turn of the 1890s, he turned themes of decadence, duplicity, and beauty into his only novel, The Picture of Dorian Gray (1890).

The opportunity to construct aesthetic details precisely, and combine them with larger social themes, drew Wilde to write drama. He wrote Salome (1891) in French in Paris. He produced 4 society comedies making him one of the most successful playwrights of late Victorian London. His masterpiece, The Importance of Being Earnest (1895), was on stage in London yet he was convicted of a crime and spent 2 years in prison. He wrote De Profundis, a long letter which discusses his spiritual journey through his trials, forming a dark counterpoint to his earlier philosophy of pleasure. Upon his release he left immediately for France, never to return to Ireland or Britain. There he wrote his last work, The Ballad of Reading Gaol, a long poem commemorating the harsh rhythms of prison life. He died destitute in Paris at the age of 46.

9. A passage from the Taoist scripture called Hua Hu Ching. The Huahujing (formerly written Hua Hu Ching) Two unrelated versions are claimed to exist, one from oral tradition and the other a partial manuscript discovered in a cave in China.

Hua Hu Ching; literally: "Classic on Converting the Barbarians" is

a Taoist book. The work is traditionally attributed to Laozi (formerly written Lao Tzu).

Lao Tzu was a venerated monk. As the legend goes, Lao Tzu wanted to leave the country to visit someone. The guards at the gate told him to write down his philosophy, to preserve it for China, before he left. He sat down and wrote Tao de Ching in one night.

Some scholars believe Hua Ha Ching is a forgery because there are nohistorical references to the text until the early 4th century

CE. It has been suggested that the Taoist Wang Fu may have originally compiled the Huahujing circa 300 CE.

10. Zen Buddhist- Japanese sect Zen is a school of Mahayana Buddhism that originated in China during the Tang dynasty as Chan Buddhism. It was strongly influenced by Taoism, and developed as a distinguished school of Chinese Buddhism. From China, Chan Buddhism spread south to Vietnam, northeast to Korea and east to Japan, where it became known as Japanese Zen. Zen emphasizes rigorous meditation-practice, insight into Buddha-nature, and the personal expression of this insight in daily life, especially for the benefit of others. As such, it de-emphasizes mere knowledge of sutras and doctrine and favors direct understanding through zazen and interaction with an accomplished teacher.

    The teachings of Zen include various sources of Mahayana thought, especially Yogachara, the Tathāgatagarbha sūtras and the Huayan school, with their emphasis on Buddha-nature, totality, and the Bodhisattva-ideal. The Prajñāpāramitā literature and, to a lesser extent, Madhyamaka have also been influential in the shaping of the "paradoxical language" of the Zen-tradition.

11. Attributed to Helen Keller Helen Adams Keller (June 27, 1880 – June 1, 1968) was an American author, political activist, and lecturer. She was the first deafblind person to earn a bachelor of arts degree The story of how Keller's teacher, Anne Sullivan, broke through the isolation imposed by a near complete lack of language, allowing the girl to blossom as she learned to communicate, has become widely known through the dramatic depictions of the play and film The Miracle Worker. Her birthplace in West Tuscumbia, Alabama, is now a museum and sponsors an annual "Helen Keller Day". Her birthday on June 27 is commemorated as Helen Keller Day in the U.S. state of Pennsylvania and

was authorized at the federal level by presidential proclamation by President Jimmy Carter in 1980, the 100th anniversary of her birth. A prolific author, Keller was well-traveled and outspoken in her convictions. A member of the Socialist Party of America and the Industrial Workers of the World, she campaigned for women's suffrage, labor rights, socialism, antimilitarism, and other similar causes. She was inducted into the Alabama Women's Hall of Fame in 1971 and was one of twelve inaugural inductees to the Alabama Writers Hall of Fame on June 8, 2015.

The Helen Keller Archives are owned by the American Foundation for the Blind. Archival material of Helen Keller stored in New York was lost when the Twin Towers were destroyed in the September 11 attacks.

On October 7, 2009, a bronze statue of Helen Keller was added to the National Statuary Hall Collection, displayed in the United States Capitol Visitor Center. It depicts Hellen Keller as a seven-year-old child standing at a water pump. The statue represents the seminal moment in Keller's life when she understood her first word: W-A-T-E- R, as signed into her hand by teacher Anne Sullivan. The pedestal base bears a quotation in raised Latin and braille letters: "The best and most beautiful things in the world cannot be seen or even touched, they must be felt with the heart." The statue is the first one of a person with a disability and of a child to be permanently displayed at the U.S. Capitol

A preschool for the deaf and hard of hearing in Mysore, India, was originally named after Helen Keller by its founder, K. K. Srinivasan. In 1999, Helen Keller was listed in Gallup's Most Widely Admired People of the 20th century.

In 2003, Alabama honored its native daughter on its state quarter The Alabama state quarter is the only circulating US coin to feature braille. The Helen Keller Hospital in Sheffield, Alabama is dedicated to her.

Streets are named after Helen Keller in Zürich, Switzerland, in the USA, in Getafe, Spain, in Lod, Israel, in Lisbon, Portugal and in Caen, France.

A stamp was issued in 1980 by the United States Postal

Service depicting Keller and Sullivan, to mark the centennial of Keller's birth.

Determined to communicate with others as conventionally as possible, Keller learned to speak, and spent much of her life giving speeches and lectures. She learned to "hear" people's speech by reading their lips with her hands—her sense of touch had become extremely subtle. She became proficient at using braille and reading sign language with her hands as well. Shortly before World War I, with the assistance of the Zoellner Quartet she determined that by placing her fingertips on a resonant tabletop she could experience music played close by.

12. Let me Love you,

    if not for the rest of your life, then for the rest of mine.
    Kaceem Madridista (13)

CPSIA information can be obtained
at www.ICGtesting.com
Printed in the USA
LVHW010004200122
708730LV00008B/151